Better
Homes
and Gardens®

Perennial
Dream Gardens

Meredith® Consumer Marketing
Des Moines, Iowa

Better Homes and Gardens®
Perennial Dream Gardens

Editors: David Speer, Karen Weir-Jimerson
Writers: Sally Finder-Koziol, Megan McConnell Hughes,
    Renee Freemon Mulvihill, Anne Nieland, Sarah Wolf
Photographers: Matthew Benson, Stephen Cridland, Richard Felber,
    Ed Gohlich, Jon Jensen, Michael Jensen, Pete Krumhardt, Sherry
    Lubic, David McDonald, Alison Miksch, Alise O'Brien

Meredith Corporation Consumer Marketing
Senior Vice President, Consumer Marketing: David Ball
Consumer Product Marketing Director: Steve Swanson
Consumer Marketing Product Manager: Amanda Werts
Business Director: Ton Clingman
Associate Director, Production: Alan Rodruck

Waterbury Publications, Inc.
Editorial Director: Lisa Kingsley
Creative Director: Ken Carlson
Associate Editor: Tricia Laning, Mary Williams
Associate Design Director: Doug Samuelson, Bruce Yang
Production Assistant: Kim Hopkins, Mindy Samuelson
Contributing Copy Editors: Terri Fredrickson, Gretchen Kauffman, Peg Smith
Contributing Indexer: Elizabeth T. Parson

Better Homes and Gardens® **Magazine**
Editorial Director: Gayle Goodson Butler
Executive Editor: Kitty Morgan
Managing Editor: Lamont D. Olson
Art Director: Michael D. Belknap
Garden Group Editorial Leader: Doug Jimerson
Deputy Editor: Eric Liskey
Senior Associate Editor: Jane Austin McKeon
Senior Digital Editor: Justin Hancock

Meredith Publishing Group
President: Tom Harty
President, Consumer Brands: Andy Sareyan
Vice President, Manufacturing: Bruce Heston

Meredith Corporation
Chairman and Chief Executive Officer: Stephen M. Lacy

In Memoriam: E. T. Meredith III (1933–2003)

table of contents

paint your garden with color

Everyone has a dream garden. Perhaps it's a flower-filled bed with bountiful blooms for cutting. Or a rose-covered front entryway. Or maybe you yearn for a low-maintenance (but lush!) landscape that accents the area around your home. Perennials offer so many options when you're planting your dream garden. They are loyal return visitors. And most require little care. In the following pages, you'll enjoy yards and gardens from all over the country. They'll inspire you with new ideas that you can transplant into your own dream garden. The perennial encyclopedia will introduce you to the wide range of perennial possibilities for your garden and landscape. **Enjoy!**

CHAPTER 1

living with perennials

Enjoy easy-care gardens filled with color in every season. Plant perennials once and you'll be thrilled with their blooms and foliage for years to come.

romancing
the garden

Love is alive and growing in the intimate garden rooms, flower-draped pergolas, and blossoming beds and borders that wrap this California home in bliss.

Step into this garden and you can't help wondering what lies beyond the curve in the path. Often the path winds out of sight, masked by frothy stands of spotted geranium (*Geranium maderense*) or Shirley poppies (*Papaver rhoeas*) on spindly stems. The air of mystery that resides in pergolas, along with the posies that make up this great garden, is part of the plot's romance.

Romance in the garden has the power to draw visitors in and make them feel at home. As the gardener, you can infuse your own ideas of peace, joy, and love into the landscape. Take cues from the romantic ways of this blooming paradise, putting your own spin on them to transform your space into an inviting garden.

Plant with abandon. Annuals and perennials in these beds are planted closer together than a seed packet would recommend so the garden looks full. Plants also are allowed to self-seed, covering bare soil with bloom. If open soil remains, seeds of tidy, easy-to-grow plants, such as poppies (*Papaver* spp.), can be scattered over the bed for additional color.

Create pools of privacy. Grow blooming screens by grouping flowering shrubs, such as shrub roses, weigela, and hydrangea, into long hedges. Border seating areas and quiet alcoves with similar-blooming hedges and tall perennials.

Left: Roses, deemed the flowers of love by Victorians, are a must in a romantic garden. White 'Sally Holmes' and pink-kissed 'Joseph's Coat' are as lovely indoors in a vase as they are in the garden. *Below left:* A skinny mulch path snakes through this lushly planted bed. You can develop a similar look by allowing plants to self-seed. *This page:* Easy-to-grow Shirley poppies (*Papaver rhoeas*) add a delightful touch of whimsy to the garden. Scatter seeds of Shirley poppies among established perennials for a carefree pop of color.

romancing
the garden

Right: Ropes of purple Chinese wisteria (*Wisteria sinensis*) drip from a pergola that serves as the entry arbor to the garden. A vigorous grower, Chinese wisteria must be pruned annually to keep it in check. *Left:* Bordered on both sides by blooming plants, a mulched path leads visitors into the garden. A succession of perennials and annuals keeps this double border in top form from season to season. Planting a romantic garden is as simple as marrying your favorite plants with intimate garden paths, gracious getaways stocked with comfy chairs, and inspiring vistas.

romancing
the garden

Right: A symphony of wildflowers grown from seed rambles over and around an island berm supported by an informal rock wall. Visit your county extension service to learn which wildflowers thrive in your area and how to grow them successfully. **Below:** Shaded areas, such as this cove, are stocked with color. Pink and white impatiens, the power bloomers of the shade garden, flower continuously through summer. Warm orange *Clivia* lends a touch of the tropics, and a soothing fountain adds sound. **Left:** Fuchsia spotted geraniums (*Geranium maculatum*), **Oriental poppies** (*Papaver orientale*), **California poppies** (*Eschscholzia californica*), **Shirley poppies** (*Papaver rhoeas*), **and white daisies** (*Leucanthemum paludosum*) **line a path to an arbor covered with vigorous 'America' climbing roses.**

This photo: Yews clipped into curves reminiscent of octopus tentacles create planting pockets for salvia. Yellow daylilies provide a counterpoint to the green and blue tones. *Right:* Flowers usually associated with cottage style temper the formal lines of the garden. Yellow and orange lilies are backed by daisies, which in turn gain context from a tall backdrop of hollyhocks. Mixing informal plantings into an essentially formal garden plan creates surprises. And it's just plain fun!

soft-focus formality

Going formal usually puts the emphasis on straight lines and square corners. This garden takes a formal base and seeks the softer side by knocking off the hard edges.

Creating an eye-catching combination of formal and informal elements in a garden can be much more of a challenge than picking a particular style and playing by the rules. This doesn't have to be hard; it's all a matter of balance. Once you decide which is going to dominate, all you do is pick counterpoints from the other style.

Introduce color with paint. In a planting scheme that relies heavily on green, white fences, gates, or arbors set off the greens. If you introduce showy cottage blooms to such a scheme, keep the color palette simple in the sea of green. Yellows work well in an otherwise green garden, as do blues and purples. Use oranges or reds sparingly; keep the more riotous colors as exclamation points in a serene space.

soft focus
formality

This photo: A color scheme of white and French blue for the surrounding structures contrasts with the green in the plantings. Green grows between the pavers and is layered from the ground up. Ivy nestles at the base of boxwoods and twines up the trees. Hostas and hydrangeas fill out the green theme.
Right: This patio area achieves a level of sophistication without falling over into stuffiness. Usually associated with cottage style, white Adirondack chairs settle nicely into a seating area with a formal feel. Clipped boxwoods swoop and curve throughout while yellow daylilies brighten the plantings without overpowering.

Bring formality with boxwoods. Squared and clipped boxwood adds instant formality. Curves work well, too, as long as they are gentle and tie in with the rest of the shapes in the garden. Keep the formal elements simple if you're going to mix in cottage plantings and accents.

Mix formal and cottage accents. Chairs and statuary can be mixed in the same space, as long as you have something that unifies all the pieces. Paint them the same color, let them all weather to a rustic patina, or use similar shapes to tie the effect together. Using accent pieces in pairs gives a balanced and symmetrical feel to the garden or patio.

Above: A gate that might lead to a French château is a welcome way to invite visitors to this Illinois garden. Opening the upper part of the gate offers a glimpse of what awaits inside. *Right:* This house and garden give the impression that they could sit in the Normandy countryside of France. The effect is heightened by the blue shutters, slate roofs, and "aged" painted brick.

room for
relaxation

Comfortable garden rooms lend welcome definition to this packed-with-color landscape.

arge properties offer lots of gardening opportunities—if you can figure out where to start. The lessons from this Kansas garden can help you lend definition to a larger-than-usual space.

Create an idea file. Before you start digging, gather ideas from magazines and catalogs. When you meet with a garden designer or start to put your own ideas on paper, you will have specific plants and designs to work with. The process also clarifies your desires and makes it easier to convey ideas to a designer or come up with your own planting plan.

This photo: A mix of old-fashioned flowers and herbs flourishes in a sheltered garden on the south side of the house. *Left:* Roses and *Scabiosa* add soft notes of color along a garden path.

room for
relaxation

This photo: Adirondack chairs look right at home in this laid-back garden—and they give the family cat a comfortable perch. *Left:* Fragrant 'Mary Rose' and 'Graham Thomas' roses nearly hide a rustic fence.

room for.
relaxation

This photo: Grassy pathways guide visitors—and the family dog—through the flower garden. Six kidney-shape berms improve drainage and help the soil warm up faster in spring. *Right:* Yellow and pink columbine show off their delicate blooms.

Divide into small garden rooms. This 2½-acre property once lacked definition, but now a series of garden beds creates intimate areas. When designing garden rooms on your property, consider how you enter the garden and how you view the garden from your house. For added drama, include an entrance to the garden that doesn't go through your house.

Add variety. Who says all areas of your garden must look alike? Adding a bit of structure within an informal garden can help one area stand out from the rest—making the entire garden more interesting. On this property, free-flowing berms host a casual grouping of plants, while an orchard and vegetable garden offer more formality. Near the house, a patio and limestone walls bring elements of the Tudor architecture of the home into the yard. The color palette is softer, too, defined by blooms of 'The Fairy' rose, scabiosa 'Butterfly Blue', and *Penstemon* 'Husker Red'.

color
gardens

Perennials offer a painterly selection of flower and foliage. Pick your garden palette in such colors as pastel pinks, calming blues, and verdant greens.

pretty
in pink

Pastel roses, artistically accented
by annuals, perennials, and bulbs,
lend classic beauty to this sunny
California garden.

Everything's coming up roses in this California garden.
Pink floribunda roses greet visitors at the gate, and a
mix of pink, cream, and peach roses creates a pastel
paradise inside the white picket fence. Here's how
to create a stunning landscape centered on this
treasured flower.

Accent with complementary plantings. Roses are an ideal
partner for the 100-year-old Victorian home that anchors the
property, but they might become boring if used alone. Annuals,
perennials, and bulbs gracefully set off the roses with intriguing
color and texture. Santa Barbara daisies (*Erigeron karvinskianus*)

This photo: Star jasmine (*Trachelospermum jasminoides*) frames the porch, adding to the garden's lushness and creating a natural link between the house and surrounding landscape. **Left:** *Impatiens walleriana* and candytuft (*Iberis sempervirens*) continue the pink-and-white theme.

pretty
in pink

This photo: Delphinium
hybrids and 'Bonica' roses
provide a burst of bold color
next to the picket fence.
Right: 'Bonica' roses show off
an abundance of blooms at
the front gate. Hardy in
Zones 4 to 9, this shrub rose
blooms repeatedly during late
spring and early summer.

and *Pelargonium* surround rose bushes, creating instant bouquets, while Calla lilies (*Zantedeschia aethiopica*) and rosemary (*Rosmarinus officinalis*) provide a deep green backdrop for the pastel blooms of the roses.

Weave unifying color. Pink provides the foundation for this Zone 10 landscape, from the 'Bonica' floribunda roses in front to the dianthus and impatiens that fill containers and window boxes. Shades of white and purple spark contrast throughout the garden and around the front porch, where star jasmine (*Trachelospermum jasminoides*) shows off fragrant white blooms.

Select perennials for your climate. This homeowner wanted quite a bit from her roses: long-lasting blooms, good cutting flowers, powerful fragrance, and mildew resistance. She asked local nursery owners for advice and decided on hybrid tea and floribunda roses that can thrive in the region's cool maritime climate.

This photo: The soft pink
bloom of a 'Bonica' floribunda
rose elegantly stands out
against the delicate petals of
Centranthus ruber 'Albus'.
Right: Plantings in front of
the picket fence burst with
color, thanks to a mix of
roses, delphinium,
columbine, dianthus,
and petunias.

This photo: This patio's river-rock fireplace is a favorite gathering spot in the evenings. Lavender, delphinium, and California poppy (*Eschscholzia californica*) bring color to the patio's edge. *Right:* A table on the deck offers a great view of surrounding gardens and displays a bouquet of bells of Ireland and *Agastache*.

color
harmony

Strong color sets the mood for a California garden, at ease with both entertaining and solitude.

Multipurpose areas in the garden can sometimes be a multi-pain to unify. But careful planning brings seating areas, classic hardscaping, and bold colors together. This California landscape offers lessons on juggling multiple roles for a space that is as suited for quiet daytime reflection as it is for boisterous dinner parties under the stars.

Heighten drama with color. Shades of blue cast a spell over this garden, adding a sense of mystery and encouraging contemplation. The cool palette complements surrounding foliage—while orange accents offer a striking contrast.

Link destination points. A saltillo-tile patio, a picnic bench tucked into a garden room defined by a rustic arbor, and a simple table and chairs near the house all serve as inviting spaces. Hardscaping elements throughout the garden, such as the arbor, a grape-stake fence, and meandering pathways, lead guests to the various seating areas.

This photo: *Clematis* 'General Sikorski' shows off its dramatic blooms as it climbs the fence. ***Right:*** A grape-stake fence and arbor form a rustic entrance to one of many garden rooms. Glass insulators atop fenceposts add country style.

This photo: A mixed border showcasing 5-foot-tall Peruvian lilies (*Alstroemeria* 'Red Valley', 'Sussex Gold', and 'The Third Harmonic') nearly hides the grape-stake fence. *Right:* The Peruvian lilies bloom in late spring and early summer. Their cheerful blooms create long-lasting flower bouquets.

Be water-wise. In an area where water restrictions are the norm, this garden design minimizes watering needs. Drought-tolerant (and low-maintenance) perennials such as salvia, sedum, and lavender add low-maintenance color without sacrificing style. The homeowner grouped plants that need regular watering to get the most of weekly watering allotments.

sweet
serenity

A soothing color palette
makes this Alabama garden
a peaceful oasis for all
who visit.

J ust like people, gardens have
personalities. Is your garden
boisterous and invigorating? Or quiet
and calming? Rooted in serenity, this
shaded retreat is all about
contemplative relaxation. From the placement
of landscape features to plant selection, the
garden encourages visitors to toss away their
troubles and revel in the simple beauty of
nature. Here's how to craft a similar space to
come home to at the end of the day.

Choose a simple color scheme. Warm
hues, such as red, orange, and yellow, add
energy, while cool colors, such as green, blue,
and purple, bring about a quiet state of mind.
Green is the primary color of this garden.
Accented with white and a dash of pastel hues
here and there, the Alabama garden is full of
interest even with a limited color palette.

When planning your garden, consider
emphasizing just one hue. A monochromatic
color scheme is particularly effective when
multiple shades of one color are planted
together. Pastels are popular and effective
choices, but bold colors can be suitable when
used tastefully and with restraint.

This photo: The arched doorways of the pavilion lend it an old-world look. A climbing rose scrambles up the roofline, subtly softening the massive stone structure. *Left:* Choose foliage plants for their intricate leaves to add texture to the garden.

sweet
serenity

This photo: A simple stone path draws visitors into the woodland garden, which is softly colored with pastel foxgloves. *Left:* Earth-hue stone on the facade of the house and in the garden creates a seamless transition from home to landscape.

Create garden retreats. A thoughtfully placed bench near a reflecting pool or a pergola situated near the house for easy alfresco dining encourages you to slow down and enjoy the space. Garden seating does not have to be expensive or complicated. A smooth stump or a flat rock can make an impromptu chair.

Engage the senses. Running water, eye-pleasing vistas, and sweet fragrance will all enhance your garden retreat. When you are fully immersed in a space, you'll cast your cares aside.

pastel paradise

Shades of pink and other soft hues create a picture-perfect backdrop in this Iowa garden.

Designed as a quiet escape for the gardener and her husband, this Iowa landscape has turned into a popular place for weddings, formal English teas, concerts, and other events. It's easy to understand the allure as you step into the allée of 'Brandywine' crabapple trees and stroll through the many themed gardens that infuse the 31-acre property with season-long pastel hues.

Celebrate what you love. Whether it's a favorite flower or color, embracing what speaks to you most gives your garden an authentic charm. This gardener loves pink, so she surrounded herself with it, planting pink-hued 'Rosy Lights' and 'Pink Lights' varieties of azaleas, 'Abraham Darby' and Heritage roses, and *Phlox subulata* 'Crimson Beauty'.

pastel
paradise

This photo: The purple spheres of alliums add height and sculptural appeal to garden beds. *Left:* Charming architecture makes this cozy home a perfect partner for the cottage-style flowers embracing it with color.

pastel paradise

Show off in your favorite season. This gardener delights in the gentle days of spring, so May is the month when her garden really shows off. She loves crabapples and azaleas, as well as the striking purple notes of 'Globemaster' allium and 'Jackmanii' clematis that add welcome color to her spring beds. But there's another reason she loves the spring garden. She points out that because she's just 5 feet tall, spring is the only season when she can tower over her plants.

Add garden structures. In addition to plentiful blooms, several quaint outbuildings and architectural elements enhance the garden's picturesque quality. Gazebos offer serene stopping points, for example, while a structure dubbed the Teatime Cottage is edged with paint that perfectly matches the color of the redbud trees in spring. Arbors and picket fences add to the traditional cottage-style look.

Left: **Spikes of foxglove** (*Digitalis purpurea*) **add vertical interest in the garden.** *This photo:* **As spring days dwindle, pink blooms slowly fade into darker jewel tones.**

in living
color

This photo: A charming white picket fence is flanked by a riot of color from pink bee balm (*Monarda didyma*) and lavender-color Russian sage (*Perovskia* 'Blue Spire') along one side and yellow black-eyed Susan (*Rudbeckia fulgida*), pink foxglove (*Digitalis* spp.), and a bright mix of annuals on the other. A white obelisk decorates the background of the scene. *Right:* Royal purple *Clematis* 'The President' twines its way along most of the length of fence. The 6-inch-wide blooms cloak the span in color in late spring and summer before blooming again in late summer and fall.

in living
color

No matter where you look, cheerful color bursts from every nook and cranny in this flower-filled retreat.

Getting your garden to bloom all at once is one thing. Keeping it flowering all season is a different story entirely. Following the tips from this bright garden, you can enjoy color from early spring well into the cool days of fall.

Mix it up. Choose plants with varying bloom times and growth habits. This Oregon garden is brimming with a mix of perennials, annuals, and vines that flower at different times so something is blooming almost all the time.

Snip the flowers. Many plants respond well to deadheading, a key to the long bloom time of this garden. To do this, snip off blooms that are no longer attractive. You'll not only clean up your garden, but you'll also send a message to the plant to continue flowering, extending the bloom time for several weeks.

This photo: From top to bottom, color is the story. Along the front walk, guests are greeted by a carefree blooming border of annuals and perennials. Underfoot, they'll find blue star creeper (*Isotoma fluviatilis*) inching its way between the pavers. Up high, glimpses of color come from window boxes and vines growing along the roof and window lines. *Right:* Two varieties of *Dahlia* are joined by garden phlox (*Phlox paniculata*) in flanking a copper birdbath.

Share the wealth. Cutting fresh flowers for your table or to give as gifts also promotes rebloom. Plus, you get to share a bit of your garden with friends.

Think high and low. Adding color up high and down low can give the impression of lots of flowers, even when only a few are blooming. Here, colorful vines ramble up arbors and over fences, creating a pretty garden backdrop. Even after flowers have faded, classic white structures provide a striking contrast to green foliage.

Fill in with containers. Pots, baskets, and containers are portable, so use them to your advantage. Where this garden leaves off, hanging baskets, window boxes, and pots of color seamlessly fill in with hue-rich combinations.

This photo: Arches in the
arbor structure provide the
perfect place for hanging
color up high. Comfortable
garden-motif cushions line
the swinging bench, making
it easy to relax and enjoy the
fruits of your garden labor.
Right: Large hanging baskets
of trailing annuals add
impact to this garden
structure. This one is filled
with annuals—red verbena,
white diascia, purple
petunias, and pink ivy
geraniums (*Pelargonium*
spp.)—that bloom all season.

color combinations

Bold is beautiful, so banish
blah by mixing colors and styles
to your heart's content.

Maybe you'd better check your notions of formal and cottage at this garden gate. If you're the kind of gardener who likes to pigeonhole places on the basis of this or that, it might be better if you look away now.

But if you're one who likes to mix up things a bit, come on in and take a look around. You'll be right at home in this place that blends formal and cottage into a mix that's just plain beautiful. How does that happen?

Be daring with color combinations. In this garden, a traditional mix of blues and yellows is the background, but the gardener has not been afraid to throw in pinks and oranges where it's appropriate.

Mix style elements. Add formal elements side-by-side with cottage-garden plants. And don't just try it in one corner of the garden or in just one element of your overall design. Make it obvious by mixing the styles in all aspects of your garden. Be sure to carry your mixtures through different accessories, furniture styles, and plantings.

Go with what you love. Mix styles because the elements you are mixing are ones that you really, really love. Eclectic only works if it works for you. Don't mix formal hardscaping with blowsy, cottage-style plantings to make an aesthetic statement. Do it because it makes you smile.

Left: **Blue and yellow set the stage for the cottage plantings. This time it is balloon flower (*Platycodon*) and bright yellow yarrow that create the blue-and-yellow background. That look is punctuated, though, by brilliant orange splashes from a Turk's cap lily and a bright daylily. The cottage feel is enhanced by the profusion of tall flowers. The height of the plants serves several purposes. The masses of foliage create a cool green background for the bolder colors of the blossoms, and the long stems allow the flowers to be swayed by the softest breeze and to swirl themselves into varying combinations of bloom.**

color
combinations

Left: Blue and yellow is not a particularly
unusual color combination in a garden,
but it makes a bigger statement when the
blues are bright, like this balloon flower
(*Platycodon*), instead of muted, and when
the yellows range from butter with an
orange twist, as in this gloriosa daisy
(*Rudbeckia hirta*), to the canary of a nearby
daylily. *Right:* "Style" becomes just
another word when you mix formal and
cottage looks in the same space. A fairly
conventional brick patio with formal
accessories—a centrally placed fountain
and an iron bench—takes on a different
personality when surrounded by a riot of
cottage-style plants, including nodding
daylilies and old-fashioned hollyhocks.

cottage gardens

A mix of colorful, old-fashioned perennial flowers, high-climbing vines, and petal-packed roses turns any front or back yard into a romantic cottage garden.

good bones

Blooming vines, textured shrubs, and tall perennials form the framework for this roving cottage garden overflowing with vibrant flowers and foliage.

Strong, healthy bones are important in the garden. Beds and borders without a solid framework sprawl over the landscape in a haphazard fashion. When the homeowners first put down roots on this rural Washington property, they were faced with a flat, grassy expanse. Knowing that the landscape called out for structure, they began by planting bones. Here's what they did:

Plant vines. In a couple years, easy-to-grow perennial vines rambled up simple trellises to create vertical structure. Vine-clad arbors and trellises were placed throughout the garden as focal points or divisions between garden rooms.

Many perennial vines are tenacious climbers, scrambling up structures on their own. Some easy-to-grow perennial flowering vines include *Clematis*, *Wisteria*, honeysuckle (*Lonicera* spp.), and silver lace vine (*Fallopia aubertii*).

Create living screens. Whether called upon to obscure an unpleasant view or create a living wall for a garden room, texture and color are tops when selecting shrubs and tall perennials. Combine a variety of textures, such as the petite leaves of boxwood (*Buxus* spp.) paired with the spiky, straplike leaves of *Crocosmia*, for a pleasing planting. Rely on repetition when selecting the foliage and flower color of shrubs and tall perennials. Chartreuse-hue perennials, vines, and shrubs tie this garden together.

This photo: Painted blue-gray, the potting shed is surrounded by a showcase of texture-rich, fragrant herbs. Five vines scramble up the trellis framing the shed entry—two clematis, a honeysuckle, a jasmine, and a silver-vein creeper. *Top left:* A bird feeder anchored in an old washtub is a lofty focal point in one corner of the garden. *Bottom left: Clematis* 'Mme. Julia Correvon' twines through a golden hops vine (*Humulus lupulus*). The chartreuse hue of the hops vine is repeated throughout the garden. These brightly lit plants glow when planted alongside dark foliage.

Left: An oakleaf hydrangea (*Hydrangea quercifolia*) and two other hydrangeas create a colorful screen beside the garden shed. Ornamental shrubs, such as these hydrangeas, are garden all-stars, providing structure and color. *This photo:* The herb garden in the foreground is divided into quadrants with the help of sheared dwarf boxwood hedges. A clipped hemlock hedge separates the herb garden from the house. With little or no grade change around the house, shrubs and tall perennials are handy for dividing the expansive space into intimate garden rooms.

cottage delights

Overflowing with flowers of every size and steeped in sweet fragrance, cottage gardens delight the senses.

t's easy to understand why cottage gardens are wildly popular. Who wouldn't revel in being surrounded by masses of blooming plants from spring until frost? Each garden bears its gardeners' personal stamp, but most have common attributes.

A free-flowing attitude. Meticulous planting plans go by the wayside. Drifts of long-blooming plants ebb and flow through the garden, creating waves of color. Plants often self-sow in a crazy quilt of flowers.

Simple and cozy retreats. Enjoy bountiful blooms in the garden by tucking a bench under an arbor or clustering three chairs near a border that's bursting with color. Visit antiques stores and flea markets to find chairs and benches made of wicker, wrought iron, and wood.

This photo: Climbing roses 'Blue Magenta' and *Rosa moschata* drape a simple wood arbor with blooms each June in this Oregon garden. Pergolas, obelisks, and arbors are excellent structures for supporting upwardly mobile roses and flowering vines.

Left: An unusual combination of peach and pink blooms together in pastel beauty. 'Westerland' rose and hardy *Geranium* 'Wargrave Pink' are just two of the many colorful blooms that bedeck this garden. Cottage style is rich in color—from pastels to vibrant hues. Choose a color palette that suits you and use it as a guide when selecting flowers.

cottage delights

This photo: Ox-eye daisies (*Leucanthemum vulgare*), catmint (*Nepeta* 'Six Hills Giant'), *Oenothera*, and *Geranium psilostemon* color this border from early summer until frost. *Right:* Easy-to-grow annuals pink mallow (*Lavatera trimestris* 'Silver Cup') and yellow California poppies (*Eschscholzia californica*) mingle in a garden bed. Encourage the duo to self-sow by not cultivating the planting area between growing seasons.

This photo: Form and function meet in this arbor as it frames a pretty view of the house and provides structure for the climbing rose. *Right:* The still-tight buds flanking the open rose reveal that weeks of bloom are ahead for this bush.

cottage charm

Bountiful blossoms and striking structures in this Missouri landscape create a gracious garden.

Great cottage gardens appear to have sprung up on their own. Self-seeding plants mingle with abandon, popping up to create a garden full of come-again color. At the same time, roses ramble through planting beds and over arbors while massive hydrangea hedges bow with blooms. This delightful look is achieved with a touch of happenstance and some thoughtful garden design. Here are a few design tips that will give your garden the carefree cottage look.

Mix it up. Annuals, perennials, shrubs, and small trees coexist in a cottage garden. Mix your favorite plants from each group for a striking display of color, shape, and texture. Shrubs, such as boxwood and yew, are not typically thought of when it comes to cottage gardens, but their shape and great looks add year-round color and loose structure.

After entering the garden through the white arbor, visitors are enveloped in a floral embrace. Yellow daylilies, pink phlox, and pink and white coneflowers bloom in the foreground while roses, butterfly bushes, and cosmos decorate the far side of the garden.

This photo: Cool colors—purples, blues, and greens—dominate the water garden. The result is a restful retreat.
Right: Blue flag (*Iris versicolor*) is a water iris that thrives when planted in the pond. Other irises, such as Japanese and Siberian, grow in well-drained soil along the margin of the pond.

Add structure with garden accents. A picket fence, a graceful arbor, and an obelisk all say "cottage garden" at first glance. Take advantage of the form and function of garden accents by wrapping your patch in a pleasing picket fence or framing an entry with an arbor. **Don't forget fragrance.** For supreme enjoyment of a space, involve as many senses as possible. Enthrall the sense of smell with fragrant flowers and foliage. Old-fashioned roses perfume the garden with classic cottage smells. Lavender, thyme, basil, and many other herbs boast fragrant foliage.

Above: Surrounded by a hydrangea hedge, this moss-covered brick patio plays host to informal garden gatherings. **Left:** A wire basket containing clay pots serves as functional garden art. A pink rose climbs a trellis in the background, offering hints of welcome fragrance and color. **Right:** Water lilies and blue flags add lush plant life to the glassy surface of the oval-shape pond.

small gardens

Get a big effect in a small space with perennials. From front-row edgers to back-of-the-border beauties, perennials offer repeat blooms every year.

rooms with blooms

Perfume-rich climbing roses, lush stands of boxwood and laurel, and rustic brick paths divvy up a simple suburban backyard into a series of intimate garden rooms.

Designing a garden is similar to drawing up plans for a house. Just as you create spaces for certain tasks, such as a kitchen for preparing meals and a bedroom for sleeping, your garden has rooms too. Create an outdoor dining room just beyond your back door, or group Adirondack chairs with a side table to create a cozy outdoor living room.

In the garden, dense green hedges and blossoming stands of flowers become walls; vibrant green grass, pebbles, and chunks of stone make floors; and a rich blue sky creates a never-ending ceiling.

Building outdoor rooms begins with delineating the space. A sprawling backyard can become an intimate oasis with a few well-placed structures, plants, and paths.

Add structures. Fences, pergolas, and walls instantly define spaces. White picket fences cloaked with fragrant roses define the edges of several flower-filled rooms in this garden. A white pergola, complete with a double swing, creates a quiet nook for reading and relaxing.

Plant living screens. Tall and short hedges and clumps of flowering perennials form lovely walls that change with the seasons.

Lay paths. A simple pebble path or a brick or stone walkway can easily separate areas at ground level while leading visitors from one garden room to another.

This photo: Bold Asiatic lilies, clusters of white phlox (*Phlox paniculata*), lacy burgundy leaves of Japanese maple (*Acer palmatum*), and airy wands of *Verbena bonariensis* all boast eye-pleasing texture. United by a color palette rich in magenta, red, purple, and shades of green, this garden shows its warm and soothing personality. *Above left:* 'Simplicity' roses soften a white picket fence and create a boundary on one side of the garden. *Bottom left:* Antique black urns planted with *Dracaena* denote the entrance to the patio and dining area beyond.

rooms
with blooms

This photo: A *Wisteria*-clad pergola borders one side of the home and reveals lovely views of the garden beyond. A brick path extending from the pergola leads visitors to a garden swing across the way and, along with the paired boxwood hedges (*Buxus sempervirens*), visually divides areas of the garden. *Right:* Asiatic lilies (*Lilium* spp.), blooming althaea (*Althaea cannabina*), and sculptural bear's breeches (*Acanthus spinosus*) create a dense, color-rich living screen to separate the shady pergola sitting area from the bright and sunny brick patio. Although the lilies will drop their blooms, the althaea and bear's breeches will display colorful petals for most of the summer.

rooms
with blooms

Once an expanse of grass with a couple of raised beds, this suburban backyard was carved into nooks for dining, relaxing, and planting. A brick pathway separates the formal herb garden in the background from the curvaceous perennial islands.

rooms
with blooms

Left: Magenta hollyhocks and soft yellow roses mingle to create a blooming wall. Plant your own flower-festooned living screens by selecting stately perennials and annuals for the task. Perennials prized for their penchant of providing privacy include **butterfly bush** (*Buddleja* spp.), **maiden grass** (*Miscanthus sinensis* 'Gracillimus'), **perennial sunflower** (*Heliopsis* 'Summer Sun'), **Joe Pye weed** (*Eupatorium purpureum*), **and phlox** (*Phlox paniculata*). *Below:* A patch of grass forms a calm green sea perfect for sipping lemonade or relaxing with a favorite book. Bordered by tall hedges and imposing perennials, this quiet garden getaway is shielded from prying eyes. *Right:* There is a rose for almost any landscape situation. This light pink beauty is planted in mass to form a hedge.

This photo: Neatly sheared dwarf boxwoods define modest foundation beds, which lend visual interest near the front door without overpowaering the low-slung house. *Right:* Plants of varying heights create an eye-catching composition in this mixed border.

high
drama

If space is limited, look up. This garden's vertical structures and plantings maximize the visual impact of every inch.

The sky's the limit in this Massachusetts garden. Foxglove grows 8 feet tall, and lysimachia, sage, globe thistle, and rose campion soar. This garden keeps things looking up by combining tall perennials and annuals with vigorous climbers. Here are some ways you can maximize interest in your garden—whatever its size.

Play with scale. Because this house sits so low on the lot, wide foundation plantings, such as yews and junipers, might have overwhelmed it. Instead, staggered layers of plantings, including clematis, fire thorn, and roses, build interest and add welcome height without becoming too massive. Sheared dwarf boxwoods neatly define each bed.

drama

An arbor framed by 'Joseph's Coat' roses and casual groupings of tall plants, such as foxglove and yellow *Lysimachia punctata,* make the 50×100-foot yard seem larger than its dimensions suggest. White chrysanthemum, daisies, and pink roses lend additional color.

high drama

Add contrast. Plantings of various colors give this small garden pizzazz as colors interact and each plant shows off the next one's beauty. For example, blue-violet *Salvia × superba* 'May Night' and the blue hues of 4-foot-tall globe thistle (*Echinops*) contrast sweetly with golden-yellow blooms of lysimachia. Similarly, the silvery leaves of rose campion (*Lychnis coronaria*) stand out amid the blooming beds.

Recruit volunteers. Many plants in this garden reseeded themselves. You can let plants multiply on their own or give them a little help by harvesting the seeds, drying them, and planting them where you choose. Using volunteers is a cost-effective, low-maintenance way to expand your garden, but be wary of species that tend to overrun the garden.

Right: A fish pond adds another pocket of interest within the modest-size yard. *Above:* A rustic birdbath encourages wildlife to stop by for a drink and reflects the colors of surrounding flowers in its still waters.

live.
big

Measuring 900 square feet, this New York City rooftop garden lives big thanks to ingenuity and raised beds.

This sky-high hangout in New York City is more than a verdant city oasis. Green roofs are becoming popular because of their outstanding environmental benefits. Studies have shown that they reduce heat retention of buildings, which lowers city temperatures and helps reduce air-conditioning costs. These benefits were realized in this garden due to a series of raised-bed gardens that transformed the roof into a lively garden.

Rise above with raised beds. Green up mucky, inhospitable soil with a raised bed. Soften an expansive deck or patio by creating beds in the midst of the gathering space as well as on its outer edges.

Above: Cedar planting boxes form raised-bed gardens around the rooftop retreat.
Left: A large cedar pergola defines the dining space, which includes a barbecue area with a slate countertop and storage for accessories.

Enjoy more plants per square foot. Raised-bed gardening eliminates the need for paths and walkways, allowing you to plant more densely—useful in a small space such as a rooftop. And dense planting translates to more color in a perennial box and more produce from a vegetable garden.

Extend the garden season. The elevated beds allows the soil in them to warm more quickly in the spring, giving you a jump-start on planting early-season vegetable crops, such as lettuce, radishes, and peas. Because of their flat surface, raised beds are easy to top with a cold frame or planting fabric to extend the gardening season on each end.

This photo: The vine-covered trellis and lush gardens keep thoughts of the city miles away when you're nestled in this quiet nook. *Left:* Low-maintenance annuals, perennials, trees, and shrubs that can take the heat and high winds that come with living 10 stories above ground fill the beds.

petite retreat

A small, barren yard was transformed into a delightful garden room: The more the gardeners added, the more livable and restful it became.

Once only a slab of concrete and three dead daisies, this California yard became an oasis of outdoor living. Undeterred by the petite lot, the homeowners had a vision of their dream garden and worked steadily to bring that vision to life.

With the help of a landscape architect, they added a seating area, an outdoor dining room, a koi pond, and a plethora of lovely perennials, annuals, and vines.

Grow up with vertical gardening. Flowering vines, such as honeysuckle (*Lonicera* spp.), *Mandevilla*, and climbing roses, grow up trellis systems, leaving the ground beneath them free for planting low-growing annuals and perennials. The upwardly mobile plants also work to soften walls and shade pergolas.

Add stone accents. California bluestone pavers are dotted throughout the landscape, unifying the space. The patio behind the house is constructed with the lovely stone. Bluestone stepping-stones lead visitors back to the pergola, and the koi pond is rimmed with the attractive blocks.

Carve out a sitting area. A pergola shades the nook and a bench invites visitors to rest. The homeowners employed the same principle on the side of the garage. Instead of a long blank wall, a trellis attached to the garage supports fragrant jasmine.

This photo: Waterlilies (*Nymphaea* spp.), horsetail (*Equisetum hyemale*), and koi call this small pond home. Located just off the patio, the pond makes its surroundings a cool retreat on a hot day. *Above left:* Decorative details, such as this lovely gate, add refined beauty to the space. All the wood garden structures are painted white or gray to tie the space together. *Bottom left:* If you don't have an open fence like this one where the tendrils of climbing plants can twine around the slats, tack a simple trellis to the fence to aid them in their climb.

Left: Judging by the beauty of the surroundings, this outdoor dining spot is the table of choice. Vertical gardening along the fence makes the most of the small yard: Climbing roses grow on the fence, freeing the ground for asters, daisies, and fuchsias. *Above:* A simple pergola makes this corner a peaceful nook as it screens the garden from the neighbors. The structure creates shade that's perfect for growing fuchsias and *Mandevilla*. **Honeysuckle (***Lonicera* **spp.) and** *Wisteria* **reach skyward.**

shade gardens

Areas beneath trees and shrubs can explode with color and texture when you choose perennials that excel in low light.

shady characters

Make your woodland garden a shade brighter by adding a wonderfully diverse palette of plants that don't need a lot of sun to shine.

Life in a woodland clearing surrounded by tall conifers provides plenty of peace and quiet, plus a whole lot of shade— so much shade that some homeowners think a garden plan could never see the light of day. How wrong they are. A color-filled plot overflowing with shade-loving plants can be as close as your front yard.

Plant bright bloomers. Rhododendrons can be planted under mature evergreens. Add azaleas and small woodland plants—trilliums, epimediums, ferns, anemones, and some bulbs.

Bridge the gap. Fill the space between the 100-foot-tall firs and the rhodies with understory trees such as small maples. These budget-savvy homeowners bought tiny trees, which aren't prone to setback shock and will catch up with bigger trees in a few seasons.

Make an entrance. These homeowners converted a dry, weedy, sandy slope into a welcoming entry garden. First the area was terraced with rocks, then a fence and arbor— inspired by the rustic log home to which they lead—were added. *Laburnum* was draped over the arbor as a crowning touch. Now visitors follow a stepping-stone path through lush foliage to a serene staircase that culminates at the house.

Add complementary color. This garden features chartreuse and burgundy, which pop out from the mild green of the surrounding evergreens.

This photo: A vine-covered arbor shades rustic steps leading from the driveway to the house. Yellow primroses and hostas, tucked into the stairway, bring the quiet path to life. *Above left:* Purple 'Negrita' tulips and a golden 'Aurea' barberry gleam in the sun-dappled area of this shade garden. *Bottom left:* A pink form of *Oxalis*, or wood sorrel, makes a handy—and colorful—groundcover for shady spots.

Left: This Japanese maple—
Acer palmatum **'Beni
schichihenge'**—features
luscious orange-pink leaves,
which are dazzling in the
shade. The small, twiggy
trees grow only 6 feet tall.
Right: This shady entrance
border stretches three tiers
deep down the slope that
leads to a log home nestled
among tall conifers in the
Pacific Northwest. Variegated
English boxwood and yellow
shrub dogwoods brighten the
area, which features rustic
stepping-stones marking a
path to an arbor-covered
staircase.

This photo: An outdoor work space charmingly displays collectibles on the far side of the pond. *Right:* A 1950s bike with a basket doubles as a container for seasonal displays. It's easy to move the accent wherever a little extra color is needed.

shaded
sanctuary

A wooded landscape and a natural-looking pond bring a sense of mystery and delight to an urban property.

As you step into this tree-filled backyard just outside St. Louis, the stress-inducing sounds of city life fade away, replaced by the gentle murmurs of a trickling stream. Rock walls and terraces installed by a previous owner blend into a harmonious whole with the soothing pond, garden beds, and container plantings added by the current homeowner. If you're longing for an escape from the hectic pace of everyday life, use these strategies to transform an urban setting into a countrylike retreat.

Add trees for privacy. Seventy-foot-tall bald cypress trees (*Taxodium distichum*) stand guard above the rest of the garden, creating a sense of shelter, adding shade on hot summer days, and gently blocking out the rest of the world.

Create a natural-looking water feature. A waterway was created out of the yard's natural slope, then wood from several dead trees was used for accents. Moss-covered logs now sit in the streambed, making the new water element look years older.

shaded
sanctuary

This photo: Stone walls and vinyl shake shingles lend a rustic atmosphere to this house and property just 5 miles from downtown St. Louis. ***Right:*** Annuals casually mix with tropical favorites such as sweet potato vine in creative container plantings.

shaded sanctuary

Accent with containers. In this garden with timeworn appeal, intriguing container plantings blend dramatic combinations of tropicals, annuals, and perennials. Containers of coleus, 'Margarita' sweet potato vine (*Ipomoea batatas*), golden creeping Jenny (*Lysimachia nummularia* 'Aurea'), and Wave petunias bring welcome color and texture to pockets of space.

Right: **Logs placed in the pond give the new water feature a been-there-forever look. At the border, large clumps of** *Gunnera manicata* **add impressive foliage to the woodsy scene.** ***Above:*** *Allium* **'Globemaster' lends its distinctive spherical form to a sunny pocket near the garden's stream.**

CHAPTER 6

gardens with water

The soothing sounds of flowing water add a serene element to any garden. From ponds and streams to fountains, water adds movement, light, and life.

This photo: One of four ponds on the property, this quiet corner invites reflection. 'Chuckles' floribunda rose adds a touch of soft pink to the scene.
Right: The tiny white flowers and delicate fringed edges of water snowflake (*Nymphoides indica*) pop up delightfully in a pond.

inviting
retreat

This Mississippi garden is true to its roots, brimming with cheerful blooms and informal character.

There's nothing like nature to soothe the soul. Having grown tired of the hectic pace of Washington, D.C., these gardeners returned home to Mississippi to share their passion for plants through their garden. Their sanctuary features a range of informal plantings and several wildlife-friendly ponds.

Embrace a relaxed atmosphere. Unrestrained forms give the garden beds a natural look, and a mix of colorful favorites pumps up the color. Pathways, sitting areas, and rose-draped arbors lend a hint of structure, but the overall mood is informal and laid-back. The planting style makes guests feel immediately at ease and offers another important benefit: There's always room in the unstructured beds for one more favorite variety.

Encourage wildlife to visit. The birds, frogs, lizards, and fish that inhabit this garden add to the spectacular show and delight young and old alike. Four ponds, butterfly host plants, and a pesticide-free environment create a wildlife-friendly zone.

inviting
retreat

This photo: Swaths of perennial sunflowers (*Helianthus*) with their welcoming yellow blooms are always a favorite with visitors. *Right:* Informal exuberance surrounds a building on the property that once was the family homestead but now serves as a place to sit and enjoy a meal.

Add a touch of whimsy. Sculptures by a local artist, including a lifesize egret, playfully enhance the views around this property. In addition to sculpture or garden ornaments, consider creating your own charming compositions from everyday garden or household objects. A wagon holding a plethora of colorful blooms, for example, can add instant interest to a patch of lawn or a bare corner in a garden bed. Creativity is the key to success—and a little takes your garden a long way.

Left: Striking plant combinations, such as this grouping of cat's whiskers (*Orthosiphon stamineus*), pentas, and zinnias, enliven garden beds. *This photo:* A wagon full of zinnias serves up bright color and a big helping of down-home charm.

filled to the brim

Water earns a cameo appearance in many gardens today; this Washington garden puts H2O center stage. If you're going to include water in your own garden, why not have a lot of it?

The dream of many homeowners is a garden filled with water. Water brings so much to a garden. The look of water. The sound of water. The atmosphere water creates. This garden has all of that by the bucketful. A large waterfall. A small waterfall. Quiet pools. A koi pond. A stream. And more. Rocks. Plants. Lawns. Places to sit. Decks. Really too much to take in at a glance. You have to take your time to savor each element individually.

This photo: Cut in two by a cascading stream, a stone path winds its way through the contoured backyard. Blue star creeper (*Isotoma fluviatilis*) and Corsican mint (*Mentha requienii*) fill the gaps between the flagstones.
Left: A bench that sits against a backdrop of Japanese boxwood serves as a place to stop, rest, and listen to the water trickle. The boxwood backs up to a small deck, which provides another seating area for the garden.

filled to
the brim

Eighty tons of rock helped shape this water-filled wonderland. Rocks of various sizes and the leftover soil from digging two ponds and a stream made dramatic elevation changes possible. What had been a flat-as-a-pancake landscape now includes a dramatic 3-foot drop for a waterfall.

filled to
the brim

Left: Many people put water in their gardens for the sounds it can make. Waterfalls, such as the small ones at the top of this garden, can be a perfect way to get the sound of running water. You achieve the full effect of soothing qualities when you put waterfalls or fountains near seating areas. The one that starts this stream is close to the house and an adjacent deck. *Above:* Tiny touches, such as the statue in the lower left corner of the stream, bring smiles to garden visitors. Such ornaments can be real conversation starters or, if they are of a less-whimsical nature, can enhance quiet contemplation.

Soothe with moving water. It masks background noise from the street or neighboring yards. Even the quietest of whispering brooks can make you pause to listen. Waterfalls are naturals for producing sound in the garden. They can be built to focus the sound outward. If you don't have room for a stream with a waterfall, a small fountain will do the job too.

Add reflective qualities. Water can give your garden a whole new look. Reflections on the surface of still water can make the colorful plants around your pond do double duty. Moving water creates an entirely different effect with the play of light and shadow sparkling in all sorts of interesting ways as the sun moves across the sky from morning to night.

Improve color dimension. Water picks up the blue of the sky or the green of surrounding foliage. Help the effect last into the night by submerging colored lights in a pond or fountain.

Cool off. Water affects the atmosphere of whatever is around it. It cools a summer breeze as it passes over. It's a refreshing presence, but mostly, water is just plain cool.

filled to the brim

A narrow path at the side of the stream leads to a point where the water flows into a quiet koi pond. A Japanese laceleaf maple (*Acer palmatum* 'Crimson Queen') stands next to the flowing water, just above a carpet of lemon thyme (*Thymus × citriodorus* 'Aureus'). Other plantings that spruce up the area include a low-growing conifer, a tanyosho pine (*Pinus densiflora* 'Umbraculifera'), foxgloves, roses, and another bronze Japanese maple.

This photo: Flagstone used as stepping-stones edges the planting beds. *Right:* Mature trees and vines shade the house while sun-loving plants thrive in terraced planting beds by the pool. Round cobbles are interspersed around the pool perimeter to enhance the natural feel.

planting
for paradise

Spiky grasses, vibrant flowers, and carefully positioned boulders give this pool a tropical punch.

Plants lend swimming pools a magical quality. They smooth rough or hard edges and introduce color and texture. Most of all, they give a pool a sense of place so it doesn't feel stranded in the landscape amid a sea of stone and concrete.

Most swimming pools need bold landscape plantings that match their scale. Many ornamental grasses, annuals, perennials, tropical plants, shrubs, and small trees fit the bill. In this Rancho Santa Fe, California, poolscape, architectural grasses partner with bright red, pink, yellow, and white flowers to set a tropical mood. Native shrubs and perennials that require little water make up the bulk of the landscape to minimize maintenance. However, a drip irrigation system and sprinklers supplement the meager rainfall of the arid Southern California climate.

Keep it sunny. Avoid trees that cast heavy shade on the pool or seating area, except in hot summer climates. Select plants that thrive in hot, full-sun conditions.

planting
for paradise

Arizona flagstone and boulders lend an informal flair to the poolside patio.

planting
for paradise

This photo: Spiky forms of New Zealand flax add vertical interest while lavender pincushion flowers add color poolside. *Top right:* Vibrant pink bougainvillea makes a tropical statement when planted above azure water. *Bottom right:* Climbing roses blanket the side of the house.

Jazz up the colors. Choose plants that have colorful foliage or bloom during swimming months, such as the combination of pincushion flower and New Zealand flax planted near the pool.

Keep it clean. Avoid trees and plants that drop lots of leaves, flowers, fruit, or sticky sap. Use round gravel as mulch instead of loose bark, shredded leaves, or seed hulls. Gravel will not wash out during rainstorms.

Go easy. Use low-maintenance native and locally adapted plants that require little attention.

Create privacy. Plant vines on a pergola, trellis, or fence to block neighbors' views of the pool.

Put it in pots. Use colorful decorative containers, singly or in groups, to display seasonal tropical plants. Hang baskets from posts and walls.

incline
opportunity

Steeped in Asian flavor, a screen
house on stilts makes optimum
use of a sloping yard.

A steep, wooded ravine proved to be the perfect perch
for this garden retreat deep in the heart of Texas.
Often met with trepidation and deemed unusable, a
precariously sloping yard or ravine can actually offer
landscaping opportunities to gardeners who see
assets where others see liabilities. With a little creative thinking
and a hefty dose of hard work, this steep half-acre slope was
transformed from a patch of grass and scrub into a popular
outdoor gathering space.

Take advantage of terraces. A gentle series of terraces built
with native limestone creates flat expanses every few paces down
this sloping backyard. Terraces make it easier to climb up and
down a slope, and they also provide planting opportunities.

This photo: The garden is serene thanks to the woodland preserved in the ravine and the gentle sound of running water. *Left:* Naturally rippled limestone slabs form a bridge and encourage visitors to slow down so they can enjoy the journey.

incline
opportunity

This photo: A screen pavilion reminiscent of a Japanese teahouse hovers at the edge of a steep ravine in this Texas backyard. Zen-like gardens complete the scene. *Left:* Horsetail (*Equisetum*) thrives in a shallow pond near the pavilion.

This photo: Edged with limestone, round ponds filled with water hyacinths (*Eichhornia crassipes*) enhance the Zen-like serenity of the garden. *Right:* A pipe creates a rustic fountain, spilling water into the lower pond. The running water muffles nearby traffic noise.

Add water. Water naturally runs down hill. Take advantage of this rule of nature and add water music to your space. A meandering stream, small waterfall, or pond-and-fountain-combination will add a valuable liquid element to a sloped retreat. A simple recirculating pump powered by electricity will push water back up the slope.

perennial encyclopedia

From small to tall, shade to sun, there are so many options for perennials in your garden. Meet some of the easiest-to-grow flowers.

Achillea

Achillea (yarrow): Hot, dry conditions don't deter yarrow. These hardy North American natives require little care, although tall varieties can topple after a heavy rainstorm. Remove dead flowers to encourage more bloom. The flowers dry easily for crafts.

Zones: 3–8 **Exposure:** full sun
Seasons of Interest: summer, fall

Test Garden Tip: Yarrow is a butterfly favorite and looks best planted in large clumps. It needs full sun and dry, well-drained soil to thrive. The plants will rot in wet, mucky conditions.

TOP PICKS

Achillea 'Coronation Gold' (gold blooms, 42 inches tall)
Achillea 'Fanal' (cherry-red blooms with yellow centers, 18 inches tall)
Achillea 'Moonshine' (pale yellow blooms, 2 feet tall)
Achillea Summer Pastels mix (various colors, 2 feet tall, award-winning mixture)
Achillea 'The Pearl' (double white flowers, 18 inches tall)

Aconitum (monkshood): Blue flowers are always welcome in borders. That's why you can rely on monkshood, which blooms from June to August. This hardy plant won't succumb to tough conditions. It makes a great cut flower too.

Zones: 3–7 **Exposure:** full sun
Seasons of Interest: summer, fall

Test Garden Tip: Even when not in bloom, monkshood has attractive, divided foliage that adds interest to the garden. The tall flower spikes typically do not need staking.

TOP PICKS

Aconitum 'Blue Sceptre' (white flowers edged in purple, 3 feet tall)

Aconitum 'Bressingham Spire' (violet blooms, 3 feet tall)

Aconitum carmichaelii 'Arendsii' (dark blue flowers, 4 feet tall, sturdy flower stalks)

Aconitum 'Eleanor' (white flowers with delicate blue edging, 4 feet tall)

Agastache (anise hyssop): Aromatic foliage and tall spikes of pink or blue flowers make anise hyssop a Test Garden favorite. These rugged North American native plants resist heat and drought and look good through the end of the season. They also attract hummingbirds and butterflies.

Zones: 5–9 **Exposure:** full sun
Seasons of Interest: summer, fall

Test Garden Tip: For best effect, plant anise hyssop in groups of three or more. The anise-scented flowers work well in fresh and dried arrangements.

┌─ **TOP PICKS** ──────────────────────────────

Agastache foeniculum (lavender-blue flowers, 5 feet tall)

Agastache foeniculum 'Golden Jubilee' (spikes of lavender flowers with golden foliage, 20 inches tall)

Agastache foeniculum 'Blue Fortune' (heat-resistant, good choice for Southern gardens, 3 feet tall with lavender flower spikes)

└──

Ajuga (bugleweed): Brighten shady corners of your garden with bugleweed. This little groundcover offers colorful foliage and flowers. It prefers a rich, slightly moist soil and will slowly carpet an area with color.

Zones: 3–8 **Exposure:** shade/partial shade
Seasons of Interest: spring, summer, fall

Test Garden Tip: Bugleweed also works well as a container plant; mix it in pots with other shade-loving perennials and annuals.

TOP PICKS

Ajuga reptans (dark green leaves, 6 inches tall, blue flower spikes in early summer)
Ajuga reptans 'Catlin's Giant' (large purple leaves, blue flowers, spreads quickly)
Ajuga reptans 'Chocolate Chip' (narrow chocolate-color foliage, blue flowers in spring)
Ajuga reptans 'Pink Elf' (compact green leaves, pink flowers)
Ajuga reptans 'Silver Beauty' (green-and-white leaves)

Alcea (hollyhock): No cottage garden would be complete without a generous helping of hollyhocks. Growing 6 to 8 feet tall, these stately bloomers come in a wide range of colors in single and double forms. They prefer hot, sunny weather and rich, well-drained soil.

Zones: 3–8 **Exposure:** full sun
Season of Interest: summer

Test Garden Tip: Biennials, hollyhocks grow foliage one year, bloom the next, and then die. Sow new seeds each year to ensure a constant supply of flowers. The plants will also self-seed, so you can dig and transplant seedlings to new locations in the garden.

┌─ **TOP PICKS** ─────────────────────────────

Alcea 'Chater's Double' (many colors, 8 feet tall)

Alcea ficifolia (yellow blooms, 8 feet tall)

Alcea rugosa (yellow flowers, 6–7 feet tall, disease-resistant)

Alcea 'Single Mix' (old-fashioned single flowers, 6–8 feet tall)

Alcea 'Watchman' (black blooms, 6 feet tall)

Alchemilla (lady's mantle): Treasured
for its soft, velvety foliage, lady's mantle also offers small, yellow-green star-shape flowers in late spring. This eye-catching perennial makes an excellent edging plant.

Zones: 3–8 **Exposure:** sun/partial shade
Seasons of Interest: spring, summer, fall

Test Garden Tip: Plant lady's mantle alongside a garden path, where you can easily enjoy its wonderful foliage. After a rain or heavy dew, the felty surface of the leaves captures water droplets. This plant makes a great companion for spring-flowering bulbs such as narcissus and species tulips.

┌─ **TOP PICKS** ─────────────────────────────────

Alchemilla alpina (silvery foliage, compact plant that rarely grows over 6 inches tall)
Alchemilla erythropoda (blue-green leaves, 12 inches tall)
Alchemilla mollis (gray-green leaves, yellow flowers, 2 feet tall)

Allium (flowering onion): Plant these hardy perennial bulbs in autumn to enjoy ball-shape flowers in early summer. Choose from low-growing rock-garden varieties and towering giants. Once established, alliums are animal-, disease-, and insect-resistant.

Zones: varies **Exposure:** full sun
Seasons of Interest: spring, summer

Test Garden Tip: Try interplanting the tall *Allium* 'Globemaster' with a rugosa rose such as 'Frau Dagmar Hartopp'. The bold *Allium* flowers pop up through the rose foliage and are a perfect complement to the rose's soft pink single blooms.

TOP PICKS

Allium cristophii (giant purple blooms, 15 inches tall, Zones 5–8)
Allium giganteum (large purple flowers, 5 feet tall, Zones 5–10)
Allium karataviense (blue-green foliage, pale pink blooms, 6 inches tall, Zones 5–9)
Allium moly (yellow blooms, 12 inches tall, Zones 3–9)
Allium sphaerocephalon (purple blooms, 3 feet tall, Zones 4–10)

Anemone

Anemone (windflower): Often overlooked, the various *Anemone* species are highly desirable garden perennials. Different varieties offer various habits, bloom times, and bloom colors. All are easy to grow.

Zones: varies **Exposure:** full sun/partial shade

Seasons of Interest: spring, summer, fall

Test Garden Tip: With careful planning, you can have an *Anemone* blooming in your garden from early spring until fall.

TOP PICKS

Anemone hupehensis (pink blooms in late summer and autumn, 3 feet tall, Zones 4–8)

Anemone × *hybrida* 'Andrea Atkinson' (white blooms with orange stamens in fall, 4 feet tall, Zones 4–8)

Anemone × *hybrida* 'Honorine Jobert' (very large white flowers in fall, 5 feet tall, Zones 4–8)

Anemone sylvestris (white flowers in late spring, 20 inches tall, Zones 4–9)

Aquilegia (columbine): The cheerful, nodding blossoms of columbine are a true springtime treat every gardener will enjoy. Easy to grow, columbines prefer woodland conditions or partially shady spots. Rich, slightly moist soil is a must.

Zones: 3–8 **Exposure:** sun/partial shade
Seasons of Interest: spring, early summer

Test Garden Tip: Columbine can survive in full sun, but it does best where it's shaded during the hottest hours of the day. Individual plants may only survive a few seasons, but they self-sow generously and will spread throughout your garden.

TOP PICKS

Aquilegia caerulea (blue flowers, 2 feet tall)
Aquilegia canadensis (red-and-yellow blooms, 3 feet tall, native to North America)
Aquilegia 'Crimson Star' (crimson-and-white flowers, 2 feet tall)
Aquilegia McKana Hybrids (large flowers, many colors, 3 feet tall)

Artemisia (wormwood):
While other perennials come in and out of bloom, wormwood remains charming because of its soft silver foliage all season long. Wormwood is available in a variety of forms and sizes to fit nearly any garden.

Zones: 3–8 **Exposure:** full sun

Seasons of Interest: spring, summer, fall

Test Garden Tip: Some wormwoods can become invasive, so it's best to plant them where their roots can be contained by pathway edgings or walls.

┌─ **TOP PICKS** ───

Artemisia lactiflora 'Guizhou' (creamy white flowers in late summer, purple stems, 5 feet tall)

Artemisia ludoviciana 'Valerie Finnis' (grayish-white felty foliage, 2 feet tall)

Artemisia 'Powis Castle' (lacy silver leaves, 2 feet tall)

Artemisia schmidtiana (ferny silvery foliage on 12-inch plants, often called silvermound wormwood)

Asclepias (butterfly weed): This is one perennial butterflies flock to. Its blooms offer nectar for adult butterflies, and it has tasty foliage for monarch butterfly caterpillars. Tolerant of hot, dry conditions, this North American native plant provides plenty of late-summer color in the garden.

Zones: 5–8 **Exposure:** sun
Seasons of Interest: summer, fall

Test Garden Tip: Butterfly weed is a tough, durable plant, but it can be hard to get established. Overwatering is the No. 1 reason these plants fail when first planted.

---TOP PICKS---

Asclepias incarnata (pale pinkish blooms, 4 feet tall, likes moist conditions)

Asclepias incarnata 'Ice Ballet' (white blooms on 4-foot plants, likes moist soil)

Asclepias speciosa (purple-pink flowers, 30 inches tall)

Asclepias tuberosa (bold orange flowers, 3 feet tall, slow to break dormancy in springtime)

Aster: For bold color in autumn, you can't do much better than asters. They come in a range of sizes that fits any garden plan. They make great companions for mums and are one of the most reliable sources of blue flowers.

Zones: 3–8 **Exposure:** sun

Seasons of Interest: spring, summer, fall

Test Garden Tip: Although most people think of asters as fall bloomers, there are a number of great summer-blooming varieties too. Heights vary from 8 inches to 5 feet.

---TOP PICKS---

Aster alpinus (violet flowers in early summer, 8 inches tall, good rock garden plant)

Aster × frikartii 'Wonder of Staffa' (lavender-blue blooms from midsummer to frost, 28 inches tall)

Aster novae-angliae (blue blooms in autumn, 5 feet tall)

Aster novae-angliae 'Alma Pötschke' (bright pink blooms in autumn, 4 feet tall)

Astilbe: Astilbes make shade gardens colorful, offering red, pink, purple, peach, or white flowers in summer. They are disease- and pest-resistant but require a rich, moist soil and will shrivel up if they get too dry.

Zones: 4–8 **Exposure:** shade/partial shade
Seasons of Interest: spring, summer, fall

Test Garden Tip: Planted in mass, astilbe makes a wonderful groundcover in shady locations.

---TOP PICKS---

Astilbe 'Fanal' (red flowers in summer, bronzy foliage, 2 feet tall)
Astilbe 'Peach Blossom' (salmon-pink flowers in midsummer, 2 feet tall)
Astilbe 'Purple Candles' (rose-purple flowers in late summer, 3 feet tall)
Astilbe 'Sprite' (award winner with pink flowers in summer, 20 inches tall)

Baptisia (false indigo): A dependable long-lived bloomer, false indigo offers eye-catching clusters of bright blue flowers in late spring and early summer. It makes a great companion for peonies and late tulips and is native to North America.

Zones: 3–8 **Exposure:** full sun

Seasons of Interest: spring, summer

Test Garden Tip: False indigo has a tendency to flop over after heavy storms. Install a grow-through peony support immediately after the plants sprout in the spring.

TOP PICKS

Baptisia australis (showy pea-shape blue flowers, 5 feet tall)

Baptisia australis var. *minor* (showy clusters of blue flowers on 2-foot-tall plants)

Baptisia 'Carolina Moonlight' (purple flowers, 4 feet tall)

Baptisia lactea (pure white blooms on dark stems, black seedpods, 3 feet tall)

Bergenia (pigsqueak): Evergreen leaves make pigsqueak a standout in a shady border. In spring, it offers pink, rose, or white flowers. The plants tolerate sun in cooler climates but are at their best in shade.

Zones: 4–8   **Exposure:** partial shade/shade
Seasons of Interest: spring, summer, fall

Test Garden Tip: Use pigsqueak as a groundcover in partially shaded locations. The leaves turn a lovely bronze color in the fall. Hardy to Zone 4, pigsqueak is at its best in Zones 6–8.

TOP PICKS

Bergenia 'Cabernet' (deep pink blooms, large heart-shape leaves, 8 inches tall)
Bergenia 'Evening Glow' (red flowers, leaves turn maroon in winter, 12 inches tall)
Bergenia 'Rosi Klose' (rose-pink flowers, sometimes reblooms in autumn, 12 inches tall)
Bergenia 'Silverlight' (white flowers that fade pink, 18 inches tall)

Boltonia: Boltonia produces hundreds of cheerful, daisylike flowers. It is tough as nails but does require some space to spread. It makes a great back-of-the-border plant and usually needs some support to keep it from toppling over.

Zones: 3–8 **Exposure:** sun
Seasons of Interest: late summer, fall

Test Garden Tip: *Boltonia* puts on a dramatic flower show in autumn but doesn't look like much in spring and summer, so plant spring- and summer-flowering perennials in front of it. Install plant stakes early in the season to keep *Boltonia* upright when in flower.

TOP PICKS

Boltonia asteroides (white flowers, 5 feet tall)
Boltonia asteroides 'Pink Beauty' (soft pink flowers in late summer and autumn, 5 feet tall)
Boltonia asteroides 'Snowbank' (masses of white flowers in late summer and fall, 5 feet tall,
   very impressive in bloom)

Brunnera (Siberian bugloss): This low-growing perennial offers beautiful foliage and blue flowers that look like forget-me-nots. The plant needs slightly moist soil and will eventually form thick clumps.

Zones: 3–9 **Exposure:** shade/partial shade
Seasons of Interest: spring, summer

Test Garden Tip: Siberian bugloss varieties with patterned foliage make great companions for spring-flowering bulbs as well as hostas and other shade plants.

TOP PICKS

Brunnera 'Dawson's White' (green leaves edged in white, blue flowers in early spring, 14 inches tall)
Brunnera 'Hadspen Cream' (green leaves delicately edged in white, sky blue blooms in early spring, 18 inches tall)
Brunnera 'Jack Frost' (green-veined silvery green foliage that looks good all summer long, small blue flowers in early spring, 12 inches tall)

Buddleja (butterfly bush): In Northern gardens, this large flowering shrub is considered a perennial because it dies back to the ground each winter. The fragrant nectar-rich flowers attract a wide variety of butterflies and other beneficial insects.

Zones: 5–9 **Exposure:** full sun
Seasons of Interest: summer, fall

Test Garden Tip: Butterfly bush is slow to break dormancy in the spring. Be patient before you consider the plant dead.

TOP PICKS

Buddleja alternifolia (weeping form, lilac flowers, does not die back to the ground each year, 12 feet tall)
Buddleja davidii (blue blooms, 10 feet tall in mild climates)
Buddleja davidii 'Black Knight' (blue-black flowers, 10 feet tall in mild climates)
Buddleja × *weyeriana* 'Honeycomb' (yellow fragrant flowers, 12 feet tall)

Campanula (bellflower): One of the larger genera of hardy perennials, bellflowers are available in many of shapes, sizes, and colors (though most have blue flowers). All require good drainage and a sunny site.

Zones: 3–8   **Exposure:** full sun
Seasons of Interest: spring, summer, fall

Test Garden Tip: Low-growing bellflowers such as 'Blue Clips' and 'White Clips' make ideal edging or rock garden plants.

TOP PICKS

Campanula carpatica 'Blue Clips' (blue flowers in summer, 9 inches tall)
Campanula carpatica 'White Clips' (white flowers in summer, 9 inches tall)
Campanula persicifolia 'Alba' (white flowers in early and midsummer, 3 feet tall)
Campanula persicifolia 'Telham Beauty' (blue flowers in early and midsummer, 3 feet tall)

Chrysanthemum:

Gardeners have long relied on chrysanthemums to provide the fall finale of color in the landscape. Available in many flower shapes, colors, and sizes, garden mums are hardy and rugged, with few insect or disease problems.

Zones: 3–8 **Exposure:** full sun
Seasons of Interest: late summer, fall

Test Garden Tip: Garden mums and florist mums aren't the same varieties. Florist mums will not successfully overwinter in most gardens.

TOP PICKS

Chrysanthemum 'Helen' (red blooms, 16 inches tall)

Chrysanthemum My Favorite series (very vigorous and hardy, several colors available, can grow 4 feet tall)

Chrysanthemum 'Nicole' (white blooms, spoon-shape petals, 16 inches tall)

Chrysanthemum 'Sweet Stacy' (peach-color daisy-shape flowers, 16 inches tall)

Clematis:

Clematis is a vigorous flowering vine that scrambles up arbors, fences, or trellises and blooms throughout the summer. These choice plants come in a range of colors, forms, and shapes that work well in nearly any garden.

Zones: 4–9 **Exposure:** full sun

Seasons of Interest: spring, summer, fall

Test Garden Tip: Clematis prefers full sun but likes its roots to remain cool and moist. Plant it behind other perennials to shade its roots in midsummer.

TOP PICKS

Clematis × *durandii* (deep blue flowers, grows 6 feet)

Clematis 'Henryi' (large white flowers, climbs 10 feet)

Clematis 'Jackmanii' (rich purple flowers, climbs 10 feet)

Clematis 'Nelly Moser' (pink-and-white striped blooms, climbs 10 feet)

Clematis 'Niobe' (large ruby red blooms, climbs 10 feet)

Clematis ternifolia (white flowers in autumn, climbs 20 feet)

Coreopsis (tickseed): Few perennials outperform coreopsis. This compact bloomer spends the summer producing a seemingly endless supply of flowers. Most varieties grow no taller than 2 feet, making them an appropriate selection for the front of a border.

Zones: 4–9 **Exposure:** full sun

Seasons of Interest: summer, fall

Test Garden Tip: Remove spent flowers as they fade to promote additional bloom. Don't water the plants too much—they prefer dry, well-drained soil.

TOP PICKS

Coreopsis grandiflora 'Early Sunrise' (award winner, semidouble yellow blooms, 18 inches tall)
Coreopsis lanceolata 'Baby Sun' (yellow flowers, 16 inches tall)
Coreopsis verticillata 'Moonbeam' (award winner, pale yellow flowers, 18 inches tall)
Coreopsis verticillata 'Zagreb' (bright yellow blooms on thin foliage, 12 inches tall)

Corydalis:
Lacy foliage and eye-catching flowers in a variety of colors make *Corydalis* a top pick for shade gardens. It likes rich, slightly moist soil. Flowers appear in late spring and can continue until fall, depending on the variety you grow.

Zones: 5–8 **Exposure:** shade/partial shade
Seasons of Interest: spring, summer, fall

Test Garden Tip: Once established, *Corydalis* will slowly spread, forming a welcome mat of color. The different types make good companions for spring-flowering bulbs as well as bleeding hearts, hostas, and other shade-garden plants. *Corydalis* is not recommended for hot climates.

TOP PICKS

Corydalis flexuosa 'China Blue' (rich blue fragrant flowers from spring to autumn, 12 inches tall)
Corydalis lutea (yellow flowers and bluish green leaves, 16 inches tall)
Corydalis ochroleuca (white flowers with yellow spots, tolerates drier conditions than other species, 12 inches tall)

Delphinium:
Cottage garden favorites, delphiniums bear towers of bold blooms in pastel and primary colors. Most varieties grow 3 to 5 feet tall, so site them in the back of a border where they won't overwhelm neighboring plants. Staking is necessary in windy locations.

Zones: 3–7 **Exposure:** full sun
Season of Interest: summer

Test Garden Tip: Delphiniums do not like hot, dry conditions. In the South, plant them where they'll be shaded during the hottest part of the day.

---TOP PICKS---

Delphinium Belladonna Group (blue or white flowers, 4 feet tall)
Delphinium grandiflorum 'Blue Butterfly' (rich blue flowers, 20 inches tall, doesn't require staking)
Delphinium 'Guinevere' (pale lavender-pink blooms with white centers, 6 feet tall)
Delphinium 'Pacific Giant Mix' (double blooms in blue, white, pink, and violet; 6 feet tall)

Dianthus (pinks): This large group includes a range of species and varieties, most of which bear fragrant flowers, gray-green foliage, and compact growth. Most are heat-tolerant and require well-drained soil. They are ideal for rock gardens and small spaces.

Zones: 3–9 **Exposure:** full sun
Seasons of Interest: spring, summer

Test Garden Tip: Use low-growing species as a fragrant and colorful garden edging. Remove faded flowers to promote additional bloom.

TOP PICKS

Dianthus 'Bath's Pink' (pink flowers, 10 inches tall, resists heat and humidity well)
Dianthus gratianopolitanus (deep pink flowers that are especially fragrant, 6 inches tall)
Dianthus Telstar Series (mixed colors, 14 inches tall)
Dianthus 'Tiny Rubies' (double rose-pink blooms, 4 inches tall)

Dicentra (bleeding heart): Bleeding heart is a good companion for hostas, ferns, daffodils, Virginia bluebells, violas, and other shade lovers. The pink or white heart-shape flowers have been popular since Victorian times.

Zones: 3–9 **Exposure:** full to partial shade

Seasons of Interest: spring, summer

Test Garden Tip: There are two common types of bleeding heart. *Dicentra spectabilis* blooms and goes dormant by late summer, while the fern-leafed varieties bloom all summer.

┌─ **TOP PICKS** ─────────────────────────────

Dicentra 'Aurora' (white flowers, 18 inches tall, fern-leafed)

Dicentra 'Bacchanal' (dark red blooms, 18 inches tall, fern-leafed)

Dicentra spectabilis (pink heart-shape flowers, 4 feet tall)

Dicentra spectabilis f. *alba* (white heart-shape flowers, 4 feet tall)

Dictamnus (gas plant): A slow-growing, long-lived perennial, gas plant blooms in early summer and provides interesting foliage the rest of the season. Once established, this perennial will last a lifetime.

Zones: 3–8 **Exposure:** full sun/light shade
Seasons of Interest: spring, summer, fall

Test Garden Tip: Gas plant is so named because on a windless day, you can hold a match near the flowers and light the puffs of gas they give off. The plant attracts butterflies. It may cause skin irritation for some gardeners during hot weather.

TOP PICKS

Dictamnus albus (white fragrant flower spikes in early summer, 3 feet tall, hardy and pest-resistant)
Dictamnus albus var. *purpureus* (pink flowers with darker veins, 3 feet tall, drought-resistant, slow-growing but worth the wait)

Digitalis

Digitalis (foxglove): A summertime favorite, foxglove bears tall stems of bell-shape flowers that are often attractively spotted or mottled with darker colors. It does best in partially shaded areas where it's protected from the hot sun.

Zones: 4–9 **Exposure:** full sun/partial shade
Season of Interest: summer

Test Garden Tip: Biennial by nature, most foxgloves develop large leaves the first year, bloom the second, and then die. The plants will reseed generously if you let the flowers mature.

TOP PICKS

Digitalis grandiflora (yellow blooms, 3 feet tall, a true perennial)
Digitalis × mertonensis (pinkish flowers, 3 feet tall, a true perennial)
Digitalis purpurea 'Alba' (white flowers, 5 feet tall, biennial)
Digitalis purpurea 'Pam's Choice' (white flowers with maroon throats, 4 feet tall, biennial)

Echinacea (purple coneflower): This perennial has everything. It's resistant to heat, drought, insects, and disease, and it stays in bloom from midsummer to autumn. The flowers attract butterflies and can be cut for long-lasting bouquets.

Zones: 3–9 **Exposure:** full sun
Seasons of Interest: summer, fall

Test Garden Tip: Purple coneflower makes an excellent companion for black-eyed Susan and ornamental grasses. Plant in mass for the most dramatic color show.

TOP PICKS

Echinacea Mango Meadowbrite (yellow flowers, 3 feet tall)
Echinacea purpurea 'Kim's Knee High' (pink flowers, 18 inches tall)
Echinacea purpurea 'Magnus' (award winner, dark pink flowers, 5 feet tall)
Echinacea purpurea 'White Swan' (white flowers, 2 feet tall)

Echinops (globe thistle): This perennial is smothered in blue globe-shape flowers from midsummer to autumn. It's heat-, insect-, and drought-resistant and thrives in poor soils. The foliage is silvery gray and spiny. This plant will not become weedy like wild thistles.

Zones: 3–7 **Exposure:** full sun
Seasons of Interest: summer, fall

Test Garden Tip: The round, deep blue flowers of globe thistle team well with purple coneflower, black-eyed Susan, and phlox. Space the plants about 3 feet apart. Use gloves when handling them to avoid the spiny foliage.

> **TOP PICKS**
>
> *Echinops bannaticus* 'Taplow Blue' (metallic blue flowers, 4 feet tall)
> *Echinops ritro* (deep blue flowers, 3 feet tall, blooms August through September)
> *Echinops ritro* 'Veitch's Blue' (deep blue flowers, 3 feet tall, blooms longer than the other picks)

Epimedium (barrenwort): Barrenwort is a favorite perennial for shady gardens because it has lovely foliage and flowers. The plants are semievergreen in warmer climates. Barrenwort is one of the best perennials for dry shade.

Zones: 4–8 **Exposure:** shade/partial shade

Seasons of Interest: spring, summer, fall

Test Garden Tip: Popping up in early spring, barrenwort makes a wonderful groundcover for shady nooks. The plants look delicate but are tough as nails. They gradually grow bigger and better each year.

> **TOP PICKS**
>
> *Epimedium* × *rubrum* (red-and-yellow flowers, 12 inches tall)
> *Epimedium* × *versicolor* 'Sulfureum' (yellow blooms, 12 inches tall)
> *Epimedium* × *youngianum* 'Niveum' (white flowers, 12 inches tall)

Eupatorium (Joe Pye weed): This
hardy North American native is virtually foolproof.
It thrives in full sun and tolerates moist soil. Joe
Pye weed blooms in late summer and early fall,
making it a favorite of butterflies and gardeners
alike.

Zones: 3–8 **Exposure:** full sun/partial shade
Seasons of Interest: summer, fall

Test Garden Tip: Because Joe Pye weed can tolerate moist soils, it's a good choice for those hard-to-plant wet spots. Use it in the back of a border.

> **TOP PICKS**
>
> *Eupatorium fistulosum* 'Gateway' (dark stems, purplish red blooms, 5 feet tall)
> *Eupatorium maculatum* (purplish red flowers, 7 feet tall)
> *Eupatorium purpureum* (clusters of purplish red flowers, 7 feet tall)
> *Eupatorium rugosum* 'Chocolate' (attractive bronze-purple foliage, clusters of creamy white flowers, 4 feet tall)

Euphorbia (spurge): Few perennial genera are as diverse as *Euphorbia*. The plants all have attractive foliage that "bleeds" a milky sap when bruised. Most are tough, sun-loving, and tolerant of poor soil.

Zone: varies **Exposure:** full sun/partial shade
Seasons of Interest: spring, summer, fall

Test Garden Tip: Prized for their foliage as well as their flowers, spurges should be planted where you can best enjoy the overall effect.

---TOP PICKS---

Euphorbia amygdaloides (evergreen foliage, 3 feet tall, Zones 6–9)
Euphorbia dulcis 'Chameleon' (purplish foliage, yellow flowers in the spring, 12 inches tall, Zones 4–9)
Euphorbia myrsinites (silvery foliage, yellow blooms, 4 inches tall, Zones 5–8)
Euphorbia polychroma (green foliage, yellow blooms, 16 inches tall, Zones 4–9)

Ferns: If the sun doesn't shine much in your garden, grow ferns. Available in many species and varieties, ferns thrive in moist locations. Plant in mass as groundcovers or singly as specimen plants.

Zones: varies   **Exposure:** shade/partial shade
Seasons of Interest: spring, summer, fall

Test Garden Tip: Ferns make wonderful companions for hostas and spring-flowering bulbs.

TOP PICKS

Athyrium filix-femina (lady fern, 4 feet tall, Zones 3–9)

Athyrium niponicum var. *pictum* (Japanese painted fern, gray foliage with ruby veining, 12 inches tall, Zones 4–8)

Matteuccia struthiopteris (ostrich fern, light green arching fronds, 66 inches tall, Zones 3–8)

Polystichum acrostichoides (Christmas fern, shiny evergreen fronds, 18 inches tall, Zones 3–8)

Gaillardia (blanket flower): It's easy to see where blanket flower gets its name. Like a colorful Indian blanket, the plant wraps your garden in bold blooms. *Gaillardia* is resistant to heat, drought, insects, and disease. Remove faded flowers to keep more blooms coming.

Zones: 3–8 **Exposure:** full sun
Seasons of Interest: summer, fall

Test Garden Tip: If you need to brighten up a boring border, you can't go wrong with blanket flower. The colorful, daisy-shape flowers are easily spotted from a distance.

TOP PICKS

Gaillardia 'Fanfare' (red-and-yellow trumpet-shape blooms, 12 inches tall)
Gaillardia × *grandiflora* (red-and-yellow blooms, short-lived plant, 12 inches tall)
Gaillardia × *grandiflora* 'Kobold' (red-and-yellow blooms, 12 inches tall)

Geranium

Geranium (cranesbill): Perennial geraniums offer a range of colors and bloom through most of the growing season—there's one for virtually every garden. They make excellent front-of-the-border plants and require little care.

Zones: 4–8 **Exposure:** full sun

Seasons of Interest: spring, summer, fall

Test Garden Tip: Perennial geraniums are not the same as the bright color annuals also called geraniums. Those plants are actually members of the *Pelargonium* genus.

TOP PICKS

Geranium 'Johnson's Blue' (blue blooms, 18 inches tall)

Geranium 'Rozanne' (violet-blue flowers, 12 inches tall)

Geranium sanguineum (magenta flowers, 8 inches tall, foliage turns red in autumn)

Geranium sanguineum 'Album' (white flowers, 12 inches tall, foliage turns red in autumn)

Gypsophila

Gypsophila (baby's breath): Airy masses of pink or white blooms are the trademark of baby's breath, a popular florist plant. It shines as a cut flower but also is tolerant of poor soil and has few insect or disease problems, making it a great addition to the perennial garden.

Zones: 4–9 **Exposure:** full sun
Seasons of Interest: late spring, summer

Test Garden Tip: There are several common forms of baby's breath. Standard varieties can grow 4 feet high, but compact types grow only 8 inches tall, making them ideal for rock gardens. Annual varieties are also available.

> **TOP PICKS**
>
> *Gypsophila paniculata* 'Pink Fairy' (double pink flowers, 18 inches tall)
> *Gypsophila paniculata* 'Snowflake' (double white blooms, 3 feet tall, heat-resistant)
> *Gypsophila repens* 'Alba' (white flowers, 8 inches tall, creeping habit)

Helenium (Helen's flower): Here's a North American native perennial with a lot to offer in the summer border. It's rugged and disease-resistant and bears many beautiful golden, russet, and orange flowers in late summer and autumn.

Zones: 4–9 **Exposure:** full sun
Seasons of Interest: summer, fall

Test Garden Tip: These late bloomers make excellent companions for chrysanthemums, New England asters, and hybrid goldenrod. Plant in mass for best effect and remove flowers as they fade to encourage additional bloom.

TOP PICKS

Helenium 'Bressingham Gold' (gold flowers, 3 feet tall)
Helenium hoopesii (summer-flowering with yellow blooms, 30 inches tall)
Helenium 'Moerheim Beauty' (rusty red flowers that slowly turn orange and then gold, 3 feet tall)

Helianthus

(sunflower): Perennial sunflowers withstand almost anything Mother Nature throws at them. Their sunny yellow blooms are a welcome treat in summer and autumn. Large varieties can grow 8 feet tall and are not a good choice for small spaces.

Zone: varies **Exposure:** full sun

Seasons of Interest: summer, fall

Test Garden Tip: Although perennial sunflowers can survive in dry soils, they prefer a slightly moist location. These plants can become huge—division every few years is a must. Plant them in the back of the border.

┌─ **TOP PICKS** ──────────────────────────────

Helianthus angustifolius (lots of yellow blooms, 6 feet tall, Zones 6–9)

Helianthus 'Lemon Queen' (lemon-yellow blooms in late summer, 8 feet tall, Zones 4–9)

Helianthus × multiflorus (single or double yellow blooms, 8 feet tall, Zones 5–9)

Helleborus (hellebore):
Just when you thought winter would never end, hellebore pops into bloom with its cheerful nodding flowers. After the plant blooms, its attractive evergreen foliage adds interest to the garden through the summer.

Zones: varies **Exposure:** partial to full shade

Seasons of Interest: late winter, early spring

Test Garden Tip: Plant hellebores in rich, moisture-retentive soil. They make great companions for early spring-blooming bulbs. Hellebores are poisonous, so keep them away from children and pets.

TOP PICKS

Helleborus × hybridus (cream to dusty rose flowers, 18 inches tall, Zones 6–9)

Helleborus niger (white flowers, often flushed with green or pink, 12 inches tall, Zones 4–8)

Helleborus orientalis (white flowers, 12 inches tall, Zones 4–9)

Helleborus Royal Heritage Series (blooms in various colors, 18 inches tall, Zones 4–8)

Hemerocallis (daylily): Among the most reliable perennials around, daylilies grow better each year. Available in an almost unlimited number of colors, sizes, and flower types, there are daylilies that suit any garden. Once planted, they require almost no care. Bloom times vary, and with good planning, you can have daylilies in flower from June to October.

Zones: 3–8 **Exposure:** full sun/partial shade
Seasons of Interest: spring, summer, fall

Test Garden Tip: As the name suggests, each flower lasts only a day. However, each plant produces an arsenal of flower buds that pop open on successive days. Because individual blooms are so short-lived, daylilies don't make good cut flowers.

┌─ **TOP PICKS** ─────────────────────────

Hemerocallis 'Barbara Mitchell' (pink flowers, 20 inches tall, award winner)
Hemerocallis 'Frans Hals' (gold-and-orange blooms, 28 inches tall)
Hemerocallis 'Hyperion' (large yellow flowers, fragrant, 3 feet tall)
Hemerocallis 'Stella de Oro' (yellow-orange flowers over a long period, 12 inches tall)
Hemerocallis 'Summer Wine' (wine red blooms, 2 feet tall)

Heliopsis (false sunflower): In a sunny border, you can't beat false sunflower for bold midsummer color. This hardy perennial seems almost immune to heat, drought, insects, and disease. The plants can grow 6 feet tall, so place them in the back of your flower garden.

Zones: 4–9 **Exposure:** full sun

Seasons of Interest: summer, fall

Test Garden Tip: If water is precious in your area, false sunflowers are an excellent choice. They bloom even when rain is scarce and make great companions for ornamental grasses. All varieties make excellent cut flowers.

TOP PICKS

Heliopsis 'Karat' (newer variety with yellow flowers and a longer bloom season, 4 feet tall)
Heliopsis 'Prairie Sunset' (golden-yellow flowers, 6 feet tall)
Heliopsis 'Summer Sun' (semidouble golden flowers, 3 feet tall)

Heuchera (coralbells): Here's a versatile perennial that grows in sun or light shade and offers colorful flowers and foliage. The plants are generally compact and mounded and send up wiry, multistem sprays of flowers.

Zones: 4–8 **Exposure:** partial to full sun
Seasons of Interest: spring, summer

Test Garden Tip: Look for varieties with colorful or variegated foliage so you can enjoy them even when the plants are not in bloom. Pair coralbells with other plants that have interesting foliage for a combination that looks good all season.

> **TOP PICKS**
>
> *Heuchera* 'Firefly' (vermillion red flowers, green foliage, 30 inches tall)
> *Heuchera* 'Palace Purple' (rich purple foliage, white flowers, 2 feet tall)
> *Heuchera* 'Pewter Moon' (dark foliage with pewter veining, 22 inches tall)

Hosta: Shady conditions suit easy-to-grow hostas, which come in many sizes, shapes, and colors. Small varieties make great edging plants, while large ones hold their own in the back of a border. Hostas pop up early in the spring and look good right up until frost. Easily divide plants in spring or autumn.

Zones: 3–8 **Exposure:** shade/partial shade
Seasons of Interest: spring, summer, fall

Test Garden Tip: Hostas are ideal companions for spring-flowering bulbs such as narcissus. Varieties with yellow or golden leaves often have better color if planted in sunnier spots.

┌─ **TOP PICKS** ─────────────────────────────────

Hosta 'August Moon' (yellow foliage, white flowers, can take some sun, 20 inches tall)
Hosta 'Francee' (deep green leaves with white margins, lavender flowers, 22 inches tall)
Hosta 'Frances Williams' (blue leaves edged with gold, white flowers, 2 feet tall)
Hosta 'Great Expectations' (blue-green leaves with yellow margins, white flowers, 22 inches tall)
Hosta 'Royal Standard' (deep green leaves, fragrant white flowers, 2 feet tall)
Hosta 'Sum and Substance' (yellow-green leaves, lilac flowers, 3 feet tall)

Hibiscus: At first glance, you might think hardy hibiscus would be difficult to grow in colder areas, but this rugged plant survives cold winters and still produces dinner-plate-size flowers every summer. Hibiscus plants need a lot of room to spread out.

Zones: 5–10 **Exposure:** full sun
Seasons of Interest: summer, fall

Test Garden Tip: There are two general categories of hibiscus: hardy and tropical. Tropical hibiscus makes a great container plant in the North but is not frost-tolerant. Plant hardy hibiscus where winters are severe.

TOP PICKS

Hibiscus Disco Belle Series (red, pink, or white flowers up to 9 inches wide; 20 inches tall)
Hibiscus 'Lord Baltimore' (10-inch-wide red blooms, 4 feet tall)
Hibiscus 'Turn of the Century' (pink flowers shaded with red, up to 9 inches wide, 4 feet tall)

Iberis (candytuft): Unlike many perennials, candytuft is an evergreen. In early spring, it bears clusters of snowy white blooms. Try this groundcover as an edger or in a rock garden. It requires rich, slightly moist soil. Candytuft sometimes self-seeds, but not to the point of being a garden pest.

Zones: 5–9 **Exposure:** full sun

Seasons of Interest: spring, summer, fall

Test Garden Tip: Candytuft can suffer winter damage in the northern part of its hardiness range. Provide a protective mulch in colder locations and don't let the soil dry out too much, especially in autumn.

---TOP PICKS---

Iberis sempervirens (white flowers in late spring and early summer, 12 inches tall)

Iberis sempervirens 'Autumn Snow' (white flowers in late spring, early summer, and autumn, 12 inches tall)

Iberis sempervirens 'Little Gem' (white flowers in spring, 6 inches tall)

Iris: Irises vary from ground-hugging jewels to bearded giants. They usually require full sun and well-drained soil, although certain species, including Japanese iris, prefer a moist site. Flag iris is aquatic and grows best in boggy conditions. There are also irises that prefer shady, woodland conditions. Bearded iris comes in almost unlimited colors and bicolors; most are delightfully fragrant.

Zones: 4–8 **Exposure:** full sun

Seasons of Interest: spring, summer, fall

Test Garden Tip: For best results, divide bearded iris every three or four years. Irises make excellent cut flowers.

TOP PICKS

Iris 'Batik' (tall bearded type, blue-and-white striped blooms, 26 inches tall)

Iris 'Butter and Sugar' (Siberian type, cream-and-yellow blooms, 28 inches tall)

Iris 'Caesar's Brother' (Siberian type, deep blue flowers, 3 feet tall)

Iris ensata (Japanese iris, large purple blooms, 3 feet tall)

Iris pseudacorus (flag iris, yellow blooms, 5 feet tall)

Iris 'Silverado' (tall bearded type, silvery lilac-blue flowers, 42 inches tall)

Iris 'White Swirl' (Siberian type, white flowers, 3 feet tall)

Iris 'Yaquina Blue' (tall bearded type, blue flowers, 3 feet tall, award winner)

Lamium (deadnettle): Brighten shaded corners of your landscape with deadnettle. Although this hardy groundcover bears lovely flowers in spring, it's best known for its colorful foliage that looks good in all seasons.

Zones: 4–8 **Exposure:** partial shade/shade
Seasons of Interest: spring, summer, fall

Test Garden Tip: Used as a shady groundcover, deadnettle will eventually "pave" an area with color. It also grows very well as a container plant. Don't let deadnettle dry out too much during the growing season; the leaves may develop brown edges.

TOP PICKS

Lamium maculatum 'Beacon Silver' (silver foliage edged in green, pink flowers, 6 inches tall)
Lamium maculatum 'Beedham's White' (golden-yellow foliage, white flowers, 6 inches tall)
Lamium maculatum 'White Nancy' (silver foliage, white flowers, 6 inches tall)

Liatris (blazing star): Bold spikes of pink, purple, or white blooms top this wildflower. Extraordinarily hardy, blazing star thrives in hot, dry conditions. The tall flower spikes make wonderful cut flowers. The plant is a favorite with butterflies and other beneficial insects.

Zones: 3–9 **Exposure:** full sun
Seasons of Interest: summer, fall

Test Garden Tip: Rely on blazing star to provide welcome color even where the soil is hard and rocky. This plant enjoys dry, sandy soil that drains well; it can't tolerate wet conditions.

TOP PICKS

Liatris aspera (lavender blooms, 6 feet tall)
Liatris pycnostachya (bright purple blooms, 5 feet tall)
Liatris spicata (pinkish purple flowers, 5 feet tall)
Liatris spicata 'Floristan Violet' (violet-pink blooms, 3 feet tall, excellent cut flower)
Liatris spicata 'Kobold' (violet-pink blooms, 20 inches tall, good cut flower)

Lilium

(lily): It's hard to beat lilies for fragrance and color. The most common types of these easy-care bulbs include Asiatic, Oriental, and trumpet varieties. Plant the bulbs in spring or autumn. Exceedingly hardy, most lilies slowly spread, forming drifts of flowers. Bloom times vary, and with careful planning, you can have lilies in bloom from spring right up until frost.

Zones: 3–8 **Exposure:** full sun
Seasons of Interest: spring, summer, fall

Test Garden Tip: Interplant clumps of lilies with other perennials, such as perennial geraniums, to camouflage the stiff, upright lily foliage after the plants finish blooming.

TOP PICKS

Lilium 'Casa Blanca' (Oriental type, large fragrant white flowers, 4 feet tall)
Lilium 'Connecticut King' (Asiatic type, deep yellow blooms, 3 feet tall)
Lilium martagon (species form, many small pink or purple flowers, 6 feet tall)
Lilium 'Montreux' (Asiatic type, deep rose-color flowers, 39 inches tall)
Lilium 'Menton' (Asiatic type, orange-yellow flowers with brown stamens, 3 feet tall, robust bloomer)
Lilium 'Star Gazer' (Oriental type, rose red fragrant blooms, 5 feet tall)

Linum (flax): Dainty flowers that dance in the summer breeze make flax a delightful perennial for your sunny border. The fine-textured foliage is attractive even when the plant is not in bloom. Flax is best interplanted with other perennials.

Zones: 5–8 **Exposure:** full sun

Seasons of Interest: spring, summer

Test Garden Tip: Flax is not a particularly long-lived perennial. The plants occasionally self-sow, but otherwise, replant every year or two to ensure constant bloom. During the heat of the afternoon, the blooms often close. The red-flowering flax varieties (*Linum grandiflorum*) are annuals and won't survive from year to year.

TOP PICKS

Linum perenne (sparkling blue flowers, 2 feet tall)

Linum perenne 'Album' (white flowers, 2 feet tall)

Linum perenne 'Blue Sapphire' (sky blue flowers, 12 inches tall)

Lobelia

Lobelia (cardinal flower): Cardinal flower is a good choice for moist, woodland gardens. The bright red flower spikes are popular with hummingbirds and butterflies. The individual plants aren't long-lived, but they do self-seed easily.

Zones: 3–9 **Exposure:** partial shade/shade
Seasons of Interest: summer, fall

Test Garden Tip: Cardinal flowers' blooms are shown to their best advantage when the plants are grown in drifts or clusters. Mulch the soil around the plants where summers are hot; plants can take more sun if the soil is kept moist.

TOP PICKS

Lobelia cardinalis (bright red blooms, bronze-tinged foliage, 3 feet tall)
Lobelia 'Queen Victoria' (bright scarlet flowers, purple-red foliage, 3 feet tall)
Lobelia siphilitica (blue flowers with white markings, 4 feet tall)

Lupinus (lupine): Lupines are a highlight of any perennial border. Best grown in cool, moist climates, they have beautiful, finely cut foliage. In colder areas of their hardiness range, mulch in winter.

Zones: 4–8 **Exposure:** full sun/partial shade

Seasons of Interest: spring, summer

Test Garden Tip: Lupines are relatively short-lived, so sow new seeds each year or plant new divisions. In colder areas, locate the plants where they are protected from harsh weather.

TOP PICKS

Lupinus 'Chandelier' (yellow flowers, 3 feet tall)

Lupinus 'Minarette' (mix of bright colors, 20 inches tall)

Lupinus 'My Castle' (red spikes of flowers, 4 feet tall)

Lupinus Russell Hybrids (many colors, 3 feet tall, larger blooms than other types)

Lupinus 'The Governor' (blue-and-white flowers, 3 feet tall)

Lysimachia

Lysimachia (loosestrife): Yellow loosestrife is a favorite member of this group of plants for many gardeners. It pops up early in the spring and develops whorls of buttercup yellow flowers. Hybrid varieties are also good bets for the garden.

Zones: 3–9 **Exposure:** full sun/partial shade
Seasons of Interest: spring, summer, fall

Test Garden Tip: Vigorous and hardy, some loosestrife varieties can become invasive. (This plant is not the same as the invasive pest purple loosestrife.)

TOP PICKS

Lysimachia clethroides (white arched flowers, 3 feet tall, can spread quickly)
Lysimachia nummularia 'Aurea' (bright yellow foliage, yellow blooms, 2 inches tall)
Lysimachia punctata (yellow blooms, 3 feet tall)
Lysimachia punctata 'Alexander' (yellow blooms, variegated foliage, 3 feet tall)

Malva (mallow): A hibiscus relative, mallow is a showy perennial that blooms from summer to autumn in shades of pink, blue, or purple. It looks best in the back of the garden and looks right at home in cottage gardens. Mallow is very heat- and drought-resistant.

Zones: 4–8 **Exposure:** full sun

Seasons of Interest: late spring, summer, fall

Test Garden Tip: Mallow looks best paired with other tall perennials, such as Russian sage, phlox, hollyhock, or wormwood. Individual mallow plants aren't long-lived, but they self-sow. Plants can tolerate some light shade.

---TOP PICKS---

Malva alcea var. *fastigiata* (masses of rose pink flowers, 32 inches tall)

Malva sylvestris 'Marina' (violet-blue flowers, 18 inches tall)

Malva sylvestris 'Mystic Merlin' (blue-and-purple flowers, 4 feet tall)

Monarda (bee balm): Butterflies and hummingbirds flock to this vigorous, easy-care perennial. Bee balm's flowers bloom in a variety of colors. This is a great plant for hot, hard-to-plant locations. It can spread rapidly, especially in rich soil.

Zones: 3–8 **Exposure:** full sun
Seasons of Interest: spring, summer, fall

Test Garden Tip: Older bee balm varieties often develop powdery mildew. Plant mildew-resistant varieties for best results.

┌─ **TOP PICKS** ──────────────────────────────────

Monarda didyma 'Gardenview Scarlet' (deep red flowers, 3 feet tall, mildew-resistant)
Monarda didyma 'Jacob Cline' (red flowers, 5 feet tall, mildew-resistant)
Monarda didyma 'Marshall's Delight' (pink flowers, 3 feet tall, mildew-resistant)
Monarda 'Mahogany' (wine red flowers, 3 feet tall, somewhat mildew-resistant)

Nepeta (catmint): Catmint is a tough-as-nails perennial that seems to be in almost constant bloom. It's prized for its blue or purple flowers and its resistance to insect and disease problems. Catmint has aromatic foliage.

Zones: 4–8 **Exposure:** full sun
Seasons of Interest: spring, summer, fall

Test Garden Tip: Grow catmint as a lavender substitute if you live in a climate where lavender won't thrive. Some catmint varieties can become invasive. Shear faded flowerheads to promote additional blooms.

┌─ **TOP PICKS** ──────────────────────────────

Nepeta 'Blue Wonder' (blue blooms, 12 inches tall)
Nepeta × faassenii 'Snowflake' (white blooms, 14 inches tall)
Nepeta nervosa (purplish blue flowers, 2 feet tall, Zones 5–9)
Nepeta 'Six Hills Giant' (lavender-blue flowers, 3 feet tall)

Oenothera (evening primrose): Sunny yellow flowers are the calling card of this rugged perennial. Ideal for dry, well-drained soils, the plants bloom all summer. Some are fragrant, and most have a tendency to open after noon and remain open through the evening.

Zones: 5–8 **Exposure:** full sun
Seasons of Interest: summer, fall

Test Garden Tip: Evening primrose blooms reliably, even when temperatures soar. In some locations, certain species can become invasive.

┌─ **TOP PICKS** ─────────────────────────────────

Oenothera fruticosa 'Sonnenwende' (bright yellow flowers, reddish foliage, 16 inches tall)
Oenothera macrocarpa (deep yellow blooms, about 6 inches tall)
Oenothera pallida (fragrant white blooms, 20 inches tall)
Oenothera speciosa 'Siskiyou' (fragrant pink flowers, 12 inches tall)

Ornamental grasses:

Dramatic ornamental grasses easily become a highlight of a perennial border, especially in late summer. Drought- and insect-resistant, these sun lovers require little care to keep them looking good in all four seasons. Grasses are available in a variety of heights, colors, and forms. They team well with flowers such as purple coneflower, black-eyed Susan, and chrysanthemum.

Zones: varies   **Exposure:** full sun
Seasons of Interest: spring, summer, fall, winter

Test Garden Tip: Ornamental grasses are among the few perennials that look almost as good in the winter as they do in the summer. Leave their foliage and seedheads in place for winter interest.

TOP PICKS

Calamagrostis × acutiflora 'Karl Foerster' (award winner, 5-foot-tall plants, fluffy seedheads in autumn, Zones 5–9)

Festuca glauca 'Elijah Blue' (sky blue foliage; 8 inches tall; tidy, mounded plants; Zones 4–8)

Miscanthus sinensis 'Gracillimus' (silver-green foliage, golden flowers in fall and winter, 54 inches tall, Zones 4–9)

Panicum virgatum 'Heavy Metal' (metallic blue foliage that turns yellow in the fall, 5 feet tall, Zones 4–9)

Schizachyrium 'Blaze' (bronze foliage in autumn and winter, 3 feet tall, very drought resistant, Zones 5–9)

Paeonia (peony): Once established, peonies can last for generations. Hardy and versatile, they're available in a wide range of colors and flower forms. All herbaceous peonies grow about 3 feet tall and bloom in spring, though some flower earlier in the season than others. Peony blooms are wonderfully fragrant and make excellent cut flowers. In the fall, the leaves turn yellow and add more interest to the garden.

Zones: 3–8 **Exposure:** full sun

Seasons of Interest: spring, summer, fall

Test Garden Tip: Peonies can be left in place for decades, but if you want to divide them, do it in the late summer or fall.

┌─ **TOP PICKS** ─────────────────────────────

Paeonia 'Bowl of Cream' (large double white flowers, 32 inches tall)

Paeonia 'Coral Supreme' (semidouble coral blooms, 3 feet tall)

Paeonia 'Flame' (single crimson blooms, 26 inches tall)

Paeonia 'Green Lotus' (unique whitish-green single flowers, 34 inches tall)

Paeonia 'Krinkled White' (single white flowers, 3 feet tall)

Paeonia 'Red Charm' (award winner, double red flowers, 30 inches tall)

Paeonia 'Sarah Bernhardt' (double pink blooms, 39 inches tall, a classic variety)

Papaver (poppy): The most popular perennial poppies are the Oriental types. They have giant, crepe paper-like flowers in a range of colors. These flashy plants bloom in the spring, go dormant in summer, and return with new foliage in late summer and autumn. After the flowers fade, the dried seedheads provide additional garden interest. Poppies prefer a sunny location with well-drained soil.

Zones: 3–8 **Exposure:** full sun
Seasons of Interest: spring, fall

Test Garden Tip: Oriental poppies make ideal companions for other early summer bloomers such as delphiniums, roses, hardy geraniums, and catmint. If you need to dig and divide these plants, do it in late summer. Plant them near other perennials to hide the faded foliage in summer.

TOP PICKS

Papaver orientale 'Allegro' (large orange-red blooms, 3 feet tall)

Papaver orientale 'Beauty of Livermere' (deep red flowers, 4 feet tall)

Papaver orientale 'Picotée' (white blooms with pink edges, 3 feet tall)

Papaver orientale 'Prince of Orange' (bold orange-red blooms, 30 inches tall)

Papaver orientale 'Royal Wedding' (white flowers, 3 feet tall)

Penstemon (beardtongue): Native to the Great Plains and Southwest, beardtongue is built for tough situations. Available in a host of colors, the plants shoot up spikes of bloom throughout the summer. Most are as hardy as they are beautiful.

Zones: 3–10 **Exposure:** full sun
Seasons of Interest: summer, fall

Test Garden Tip: Beardtongue is a good companion for itself. Plant different varieties together for a riot of summer color. The flowers are hummingbird favorites.

TOP PICKS

Penstemon barbatus 'Prairie Splendor' (pink flowers, 2 feet tall)
Penstemon digitalis 'Husker Red' (deep red foliage, white flowers, 30 inches tall, award-winning variety)
Penstemon × mexicali 'Red Rocks' (rose-red flowers, 15 inches tall)
Penstemon War Axe strain (wide color range, 4 feet tall)

Perovskia (Russian sage): Russian sage is virtually foolproof, producing lovely spikes of lavender-blue flowers from midsummer to autumn, and silvery foliage all season. It looks great with grasses, purple coneflower, and black-eyed Susan.

Zones: 5–9   **Exposure:** full sun

Seasons of Interest: summer, fall

Test Garden Tip: In spring, don't prune until you see where the new growth is coming from.

> ### TOP PICKS
>
> *Perovskia atriplicifolia* (blue blooms, silver-gray foliage, 4 feet tall)
> *Perovskia atriplicifolia* 'Filagran' (blue-purple blooms, 30 inches tall, upright habit)
> *Perovskia atriplicifolia* 'Little Spire' (blue-purple blooms, 2 feet tall)
> *Perovskia atriplicifolia* 'Longin' (blue-purple blooms, 4 feet tall, more upright in habit)

Phlox: Enjoy sensational summer color in your garden with phlox, a large group of plants encompassing diverse heights, colors, and forms, including ground-hugging and tall, towering species. Most phlox need a sunny spot in the garden and well-drained soil. The plants are a butterfly favorite, and the tall varieties make wonderful cut flowers. Many are delightfully fragrant.

Zones: 3–8 **Exposure:** full sun
Seasons of Interest: spring, summer

Test Garden Tip: Some varieties of tall phlox have a tendency to become infected with powdery mildew. Spacing plants to allow adequate air circulation helps prevent disease.

TOP PICKS

Phlox maculata 'Miss Lingard' (fragrant white flowers, 3 feet tall, mildew-resistant)
Phlox paniculata 'David' (pure white flowers, 4 feet tall, mildew-resistant, award winner)
Phlox paniculata 'Norah Leigh' (variegated foliage, lavender blooms, 3 feet tall)
Phlox paniculata 'The King' (violet-blue flowers, 30 inches tall)
Phlox stolonifera (purple flowers, 10 inches tall, shade-tolerant)
Phlox subulata (red, pink, or white flowers; 4 inches tall; rock garden plant)

Platycodon (balloon flower): A sturdy, easy-care perennial, balloon flower produces delightful bell-shape pink, white, or blue blooms from late summer to early autumn. It thrives in full sun or light shade. Enjoy the balloon-shape buds before they open, or pop them open early.

Zones: 3–8 **Exposure:** full sun

Seasons of Interest: summer, fall

Test Garden Tip: Balloon flower can be slow to break dormancy in spring. Be patient before you decide your plants have died. Try planting in spring-blooming bulb beds so the bulbs disguise the open spot left by late-waking balloon flower.

┌─ **TOP PICKS** ──

Platycodon grandiflorus f. *albus* (large white flowers, 2 feet tall)

Platycodon grandiflorus 'Hakone Blue' (double violet flowers, 2 feet tall)

Platycodon grandiflorus subsp. *mariesii* (blue flowers, 18 inches tall)

└──

Primula (primrose): Springtime jewels, primroses come in a variety of colors, shapes, and forms. All require a rich, peaty soil; partial shade; and plenty of moisture. They do best in cool-summer climates; treat them as annuals where summers are hot.

Zones: varies   **Exposure:** partial shade
Season of Interest: spring

Test Garden Tip: In the right location, few spring-blooming perennials can outperform primroses. They are ideal for the woodland garden and team well with spring-flowering bulbs.

┌─ **TOP PICKS** ─────────────────────────────────

Primula auricula (fragrant yellow flowers, gray-green foliage, 8 inches tall, Zones 3–8)
Primula denticulata (purple flowers in tight clusters, 18 inches tall, Zones 2–8)
Primula florindae (yellow flowers, 4 feet tall, Zones 3–8)
Primula japonica (purple-red flowers, 18 inches tall, Zones 3–8)

Polemonium (Jacob's ladder): Jacob's ladder adds hard-to-find blue tones to the perennial garden. It has interesting ladderlike foliage and tall spikes of lavender-blue flowers in early summer.

Zones: 3–8 **Exposure:** full sun/partial shade
Seasons of Interest: spring, summer

Test Garden Tip: Jacob's ladder is generally happiest in partial shade, but the more dramatic variegated forms enjoy shady corners of the garden.

TOP PICKS

Polemonium caeruleum 'Bressingham Purple' (blue flowers, purple-tinged foliage, 15 inches tall)
Polemonium caeruleum 'Brise d' Anjou' (creamy-edged foliage, blue flowers, 32 inches tall)
Polemonium caeruleum 'Snow and Sapphires' (white-edged foliage, blue flowers, 32 inches tall)

Pulmonaria (lungwort): Hostas aren't the only shade dwellers with interesting foliage. Lungwort is an often overlooked perennial that tolerates shade and has variegated foliage and lovely pink, white, or blue flowers in early spring.

Zones: 3–8 **Exposure:** shade/partial shade

Seasons of interest: spring, summer, fall

Test Garden Tip: Lungwort makes a great companion for spring-blooming perennials such as hostas, bluebells, and deadnettles. Also try it with spring-blooming bulbs.

TOP PICKS

Pulmonaria longifolia 'Bertram Anderson' (green leaves with silver spots, blue blooms, 12 inches tall)

Pulmonaria officinalis 'Sissinghurst White' (green leaves spotted with silver, white flowers, 12 inches tall)

Pulmonaria rubra 'Redstart' (green foliage, coral-red blooms, 16 inches tall, often the first lungwort to bloom in spring)

Pulsatilla (pasque flower): Pasque flower is one of the first perennials to bloom in the spring. This hardy but demure flower partners well with spring-blooming bulbs. Plant it in the front of the garden to best enjoy its early bloom.

Zones: 5–8 **Exposure:** full sun

Seasons of Interest: spring, summer

Test Garden Tip: A good rock garden plant, pasque flower thrives in sunny, well-drained locations. It doesn't like to be divided or transplanted, so carefully choose where you plant it.

---TOP PICKS---

Pulsatilla vulgaris (purple flowers, fuzzy flower buds in spring, 8 inches tall)

Pulsatilla vulgaris f. *alba* (white flowers, silvery hairs on the foliage, 8 inches tall)

Pulsatilla vulgaris var. *rubra* (violet-red flowers, fuzzy flower buds in spring, 8 inches tall)

Rudbeckia (black-eyed Susan): Few perennials are as easy to grow as black-eyed Susans. These hardy sun worshippers are heat- and drought-resistant and bear wave after wave of cheerful flowers all summer. The blooms make long-lasting cut flowers.

Zones: 3–9 **Exposure:** full sun
Seasons of Interest: summer, fall

Test Garden Tip: Plant black-eyed Susans in large drifts or clumps for best effect. Remove flowers as they fade to encourage additional bloom.

TOP PICKS

Rudbeckia fulgida 'Goldsturm' (golden flowers with contrasting black centers, 3 feet tall, award winner)
Rudbeckia 'Herbstsonne' (golden-yellow blooms, 6 feet tall, upright habit)
Rudbeckia hirta (golden-yellow blooms, 3 feet tall)
Rudbeckia maxima (golden-yellow blooms, gray-green leaves, 6 feet tall)

Salvia: Nonculinary members of this huge group are prized for their vivid spikes of flowers and scented green or gray-green leaves. Heat-, drought-, and insect-resistant, salvias are a sure bet to succeed in your garden. If you remove the faded flowers, most salvias will rebloom.

Zones: varies **Exposure:** full sun
Seasons of Interest: summer, fall

Test Garden Tip: Few perennials bloom as intensely as salvias. Plant them in drifts or clumps for the best effect.

TOP PICKS

Salvia argentea (fuzzy silver leaves, white flowers, 3 feet tall, short-lived, Zones 5–8)
Salvia leucantha (purple flowers, 40 inches tall, Zones 10–11)
Salvia nemorosa 'Cardonna' (violet-blue flowers, 30 inches tall, long bloom season, Zones 5–9)
Salvia nemorosa 'East Friesland' (violet-blue flowers, 2 feet tall, Zones 5–9)
Salvia verticillata 'Purple Rain' (purple-gray flowers, 3 feet tall, Zones 5–8)

Scabiosa (pincushion flower): Cheery and reliable, pincushion flower is a favorite with gardeners and butterflies alike. The nectar-rich flowers appear in shades of blue, pink, and yellow and are wonderful cut flowers.

Zones: 4–8 **Exposure:** full sun/light shade

Seasons of Interest: spring, summer, fall

Test Garden Tip: The colorful, airy flowers of pincushion flower look their best when the plants are grown in large drifts. This isn't a long-lived perennial, so replant every few years.

┌─ **TOP PICKS** ─────────────────────────────

Scabiosa caucasica (blue flowers, 2 feet tall, good cut flower)

Scabiosa columbaria 'Butterfly Blue' (soft blue flowers, 16 inches tall, award-winning variety)

Scabiosa columbaria 'Pink Mist' (lavender-pink flowers, 16 inches tall)

Scabiosa ochroleuca (pale yellow flowers, 3 feet tall)

Sedum: A huge group, sedums are sun lovers that are insect-, heat-, and drought-resistant. They vary from low-growing groundcovers to taller plants that fit in the back of a perennial border. There's a sedum for virtually every garden.

Zones: 3–8 **Exposure:** full sun

Seasons of Interest: spring, summer, fall

Test Garden Tip: Although most sedums don't bloom until autumn, their fleshy, attractive foliage makes an interesting addition to the border earlier in the year. Divide the plants every three or four years.

TOP PICKS

Sedum acre (evergreen foliage, yellow blooms, 2 inches tall)

Sedum kamtschaticum (yellow blooms, 4 inches tall)

Sedum spectabile 'Brilliant' (bright pink blooms, 18 inches tall)

Sedum spurium (evergreen foliage, purple blooms, 4 inches tall)

Sempervivum (hen-and-chicks):

These plants were once planted on the rooftops of houses to help ward off lightning and witches. The plants produce stalks of bright pink or purple flowers in midsummer and form many offshoots.

Zones: 4–9 **Exposure:** full sun

Seasons of Interest: spring, summer, fall

Test Garden Tip: Heat- and drought-resistant, hen-and-chicks is the perfect groundcover in exposed locations. It's not fussy about soil but does require good drainage.

— TOP PICKS —

Sempervivum arachnoideum (green leaves with fuzzy hairs, reddish flowers, 3 inches tall)

Sempervivum tectorum 'Limelight' (chartreuse leaves tipped with pink, purple flowers, 6 inches tall)

Sempervivum tectorum 'Red-Purple' (green leaves shaded with red and purple tones, purple flowers, 6 inches tall)

Solidago (goldenrod): Colorful, hardy, and noninvasive, goldenrod is a choice perennial for late-summer gardens. The deep golden-yellow trusses of blooms appear in August and continue through early autumn. Different varieties add different textures to the fall garden.

Zones: 4–8 **Exposure:** full sun

Seasons of Interest: late summer, fall

Test Garden Tip: Goldenrod, both the wild forms and hybrid varieties, does not cause hayfever as commonly believed. Goldenrod gets the blame because its showy flowers are visible during the time when ragweed is at its worst.

┌─ **TOP PICKS** ───

Solidago 'Crown of Rays' (large golden blooms, 3 feet tall, extra-sturdy)

Solidago 'Fireworks' (golden blooms in loose clusters, 4 feet tall)

Solidago 'Golden Baby' (golden-yellow blooms; tidy, compact plants; 2 feet tall)

Stachys (lamb's-ears): The fuzzy leaves of lamb's-ears are a special treat when paired with bright color perennials in the garden. The plants bloom in summer, but the foliage is the main attraction.

Zones: 4–8 **Exposure:** full sun/partial shade
Seasons of Interest: spring, summer, fall

Test Garden Tip: Use lamb's-ears at the front of a border, where its appealing foliage can be best admired. Children love to brush the soft silver leaves. This plant can self-sow excessively if not deadheaded.

TOP PICKS

Stachys byzantina (gray-green foliage, spikes of purple blooms, 18 inches tall)
Stachys byzantina 'Primrose Heron' (yellowish gray foliage, spikes of purple blooms, 18 inches tall)
Stachys byzantina 'Silver Carpet' (gray-green foliage, nonblooming variety, 18 inches tall)

Tiarella (foam flower): In light or dappled shade, foam flower shines. A great companion for spring-blooming bulbs, this plant offers interesting foliage and flowers. Foam flower requires rich, slightly moist soil.

Zones: 4–8 **Exposure:** shade/partial shade
Seasons of Interest: spring, summer, fall

Test Garden Tip: Foam flower gets its name from the plant's foamy, white flower stalks that appear in spring.

TOP PICKS

Tiarella cordifolia (creamy-white flowers, green foliage that turns reddish in autumn, 12 inches tall)

Tiarella 'Crow Feather' (creamy-white flowers, green foliage that turns bright red and pink in autumn, 12 inches tall)

Tiarella 'Seafoam' (lots of creamy-white flowers, green foliage marked purple, 12 inches tall)

Tiarella wherryi (creamy-white flowers, green foliage, 8 inches tall, slower-growing than most types)

Tradescantia

(spiderwort): A great plant that resists heat, disease, and insects, spiderwort provides valuable garden color from June until September if it's kept moist enough. When not in bloom, the plant boasts attractive, straplike foliage.

Zones: 4–8 **Exposure:** full sun

Seasons of Interest: spring, summer, fall

Test Garden Tip: Wild forms of spiderwort can become invasive, but hybrids rarely cause trouble. They make excellent midborder selections.

┌─ **TOP PICKS** ─────────────────────────────

Tradescantia 'Blue and Gold' (rich indigo blue flowers, bright chartreuse foliage, 2 feet tall)

Tradescantia 'Concord Grape' (rich purple blooms, bluish-silvery foliage, 2 feet tall)

Tradescantia 'Innocence' (white flowers, 15 inches tall)

Tradescantia 'Osprey' (white blooms shaded with silvery blue, 2 feet tall)

Veronica (speedwell): With careful planning, you can have speedwells in bloom from spring to autumn. Creeping forms of this easy-to-grow plant bloom in spring; tall types are showy in midsummer and bloom to frost.

Zones: 4–8 **Exposure:** full sun/light shade
Seasons of Interest: spring, summer, fall

Test Garden Tip: To promote additional flowering, shear the flower spikes back when the blooms fade.

┌─ **TOP PICKS** ─────────────────────────────────

Veronica 'Crater Lake Blue' (rich blue flowers, 18 inches tall, good groundcover)
Veronica spicata 'Icicle' (white blooms, 2 feet tall, especially vigorous)
Veronica spicata 'Red Fox' (reddish-pink flower spikes, 12 inches tall, good alternative to purple loosestrife)
Veronica 'Sunny Border Blue' (violet-blue flowers, 20 inches tall, extra-long bloom season, award winner)

Vinca (periwinkle):
Periwinkle creates a carpet of color in the shade. It has evergreen foliage and bears cheerful flowers in the spring. Some varieties have variegated foliage and remain colorful all year.

Zones: 4–9 **Exposure:** shade/partial shade
Seasons of Interest: spring, summer, fall

Test Garden Tip: Periwinkle varieties make great edging plants along a shady path or under tall, deciduous shrubs. Don't confuse this perennial with annual vinca, which is botanically *Catharanthus roseus*.

TOP PICKS

Vinca minor (blue flowers, 8 inches tall, tolerates dry shade)
Vinca minor 'Alba' (white flowers, 8 inches tall)
Vinca minor 'Azurea Flore Pleno' (double blue flowers, 8 inches tall)
Vinca minor 'Illumination' (variegated golden leaves, blue flowers, 8 inches tall)

Viola (violet): A cheerful early bird, violet is one of the first perennials to pop up in spring. Happy in shade or light shade, violets are ideal for woodland gardens. Once established, they can carpet an area with color. Many are fragrant.

Zones: 4–8   **Exposure:** shade/partial shade

Seasons of Interest: spring, summer, fall

Test Garden Tip: Use violets in hard-to-plant locations where other shade dwellers won't thrive. These spring bloomers are a lot tougher than they look and will often rebloom in autumn.

TOP PICKS

Viola biflora (yellow flowers, 3 inches tall)

Viola cornuta (lilac-blue flowers, 6 inches tall)

Viola labradorica (pale purple flowers, bronze-tinged foliage, 3 inches tall)

Viola 'Rebecca' (ruffled violet-and-white flowers, vanilla fragrance, 12 inches tall)

Viola tricolor (blue, yellow, and orange flowers; 6 inches tall)

Consider Your Climate

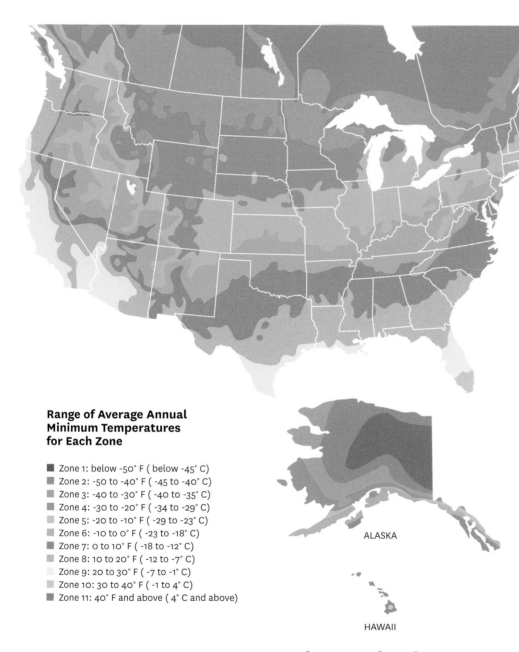

ALASKA

HAWAII

Range of Average Annual Minimum Temperatures for Each Zone

- ■ Zone 1: below -50° F (below -45° C)
- ■ Zone 2: -50 to -40° F (-45 to -40° C)
- ■ Zone 3: -40 to -30° F (-40 to -35° C)
- ■ Zone 4: -30 to -20° F (-34 to -29° C)
- ■ Zone 5: -20 to -10° F (-29 to -23° C)
- ■ Zone 6: -10 to 0° F (-23 to -18° C)
- ■ Zone 7: 0 to 10° F (-18 to -12° C)
- ■ Zone 8: 10 to 20° F (-12 to -7° C)
- ■ Zone 9: 20 to 30° F (-7 to -1° C)
- ■ Zone 10: 30 to 40° F (-1 to 4° C)
- ■ Zone 11: 40° F and above (4° C and above)

Make sure the plants you choose suit your climate. This map will help you determine your growing Zone.

Creating an attractive garden involves
more than coordinating colors and selecting eye-pleasing varieties. Aesthetics won't mean much if climate extremes wilt, freeze, or decay your tender perennials.

Climate maps like this one show low-temperature extremes by Zone. Choosing plants best adapted to your Zone and planting them at the right time increases your chances of success.

Use climate maps only as general guides, however; dozens of microclimates exist within each 1-mile radius. Even within your yard, variations in exposure and topography will affect plants. Examples of conditions to consider include:

EXPOSURE Southern and western exposures are the sunniest and warmest spots of most yards. Match each plant's needs to its proper exposure.

WIND Gusting winds dry out soil and endanger delicate plants.

ELEVATION Cold air drains from hills and forms frost pockets in low areas. Such pockets are deadly for some plants. Put plants that prefer warmth on the tops or sides of hills.

STRUCTURES Place plants near structures such as buildings, fences, walls, and shrubs where they will benefit from shelter. Pay attention to shade, wind flow, and snowdrifts caused by structures. Those varying situations are ideal for some plants but harmful to others.

A

Acanthus spinosus (bear's breeches), *85*
Accents
    adding structure with, 73, 77
    complementary plantings, 28, *33*
    in formal garden, 18
    stone, 102
Acer palmatum (Japanese maple), *110, 132–133*
Achillea (yarrow), *59,* **148**
Aconitum (monkshood), **149**
Agastache (anise hyssop), *35,* **150**
Ajuga (bugleweed), **151**
Alcea (hollyhock), *88,* **152**
Alchemilla (lady's mantle), **153**
Allium (flowering onion), *49, 50, 116,* **154**
Alstroemeria (Peruvian lilies), *38, 39*
Althaea (*Althaea*), *85*
Anemone (windflower), **155**
Anise hyssop (*Agastache*), *35,* **150**
Aquilegia (columbine), *25,* **156**
Arbor, *56, 72, 109, 111*
Artemisia (wormwood), **157**
Asclepias (butterfly weed), **158**
Aster (aster), **159**
Astilbe (astilbe), **160**
Azaleas, 46

B

Baby's breath (*Gypsophila*), **184**
Bald cypress, *113, 114*
Balloon flower (*Platycodon*), *58, 60,* **220**
Baptisia (false indigo), **161**
Barberry, *108*
Barrenwort (*Epimedium*), **178**
Beardtongue (*Penstemon*), **216**
Bear's breeches (*Acanthus spinosus*), *85*
Bee balm (*Monarda*), *52,* **207**
Bellflower (*Campanula*), **166**
Bells of Ireland, *35*
Bergenia (pigsqueak), **162**
Black-Eyed Susan (*Rudbeckia*), *52,* **225**
Blanket flower (*Gaillardia*), **182**
Blazing star (*Liatris*), **199**
Bleeding heart (*Dicentra*), **173**
Blue flag (*Iris versicolor*), *77, 79*
Blue star creeper (*Isotoma fluviatilis*), *54, 127*
Boltonia (boltonia), **163**

Bones, garden, 64
Bougainvillea, *139*
Boxwoods (*Buxus*), *16–17, 18, 45, 64, 67, 84, 90, 91, 111, 126*
Brunnera (Siberian bugloss), **164**
Buddleja (butterfly bush), **165**
Bugleweed (*Ajuga*), **151**
Butterfly bush (*Buddleja*), **165**
Butterfly weed (*Asclepias*), **158**

C

California poppy (*Eschscholzia*), *12, 34, 71*
Calla lilies (*Zantedeschia aethiopica*), *31, 33*
Campanula (bellflower), **166**
Candytuft (*Iberis*), 28, **195**
Cardinal flower (*Lobelia*), **203**
Catmint (*Nepeta*), *70,* **208**
Cat's whiskers (*Orthosiphon stamineus*), *124*
Centranthus ruber, *32*
Chrysanthemum (chrysanthemum), **167**
Clematis (clematis), 64, **168**
    'General Sikorski,' *36*
    'Jackmani,' *50*
    'Mme. Julia Correvon,' *64*
    'The President,' *53*
Climate
    map, 237
    selecting plants for your climate, 31
Clivia, *13*
Color
    for drama, 35
    in formal garden, 15
    poolside plantings, 139
    in shade gardens, 108
    in water gardens, 131
Color gardens, 26–61
    accenting complementary plantings, 28, 31
    blooming in all seasons, 53–61
    color harmony, 34–39
    color scheme, choosing simple, 40
    mixing style elements, 60
    pastels, 46–51
    unifying color in, 31
Color scheme, choosing, 40
Columbine (*Aquilegia*), *25,* **156**
Complementary plantings, 28, 31
Coneflower, purple (*Echinacea*), **176**

Containers
    in color gardens, 55
    poolside plantings, 139
    in shade garden, 116
Contrast, 94
Coralbells (*Heuchera*), **191**
Coreopsis (tickseed), **169**
Corsican mint (*Mentha requienii*), *127*
Corydalis (corydalis), **170**
Cottage gardens, 62–79
    adding structure with accents, 73, 77
    bones of, 64
    fragrance in, 77
    mixing plant types in, 73
Cranesbill (*Geranium*), *8, 12, 68, 70,* **183**
Creeping Jenny (*Lysimachia nummularia*), *116*
Crocosmia, 64

D

Dahlia, *55*
Daisy (*Leucanthemum*), *12, 15, 70, 92*
Daylily (*Hemerocallis*), *14–15, 17, 60,* **188–189**
Deadheading, 53
Deadnettle (*Lamium*), **198**
Delphinium (delphinium), *30, 34,* **171**
Destination points, linking, 35
Dianthus (pinks), *33,* **172**
Dicentra (bleeding heart), **173**
Dictamnus (gas plant), **174**
Digitalis (foxglove), *43, 50, 52, 92–93,* **175**

E

Echinacea (purple coneflower), **176**
Echinops (globe thistle), *94,* **177**
Eichhornia crassipes (water hyacinth), *144*
Entry garden, 108
Epimedium (barrenwort), **178**
Equisetum (horsetail), *103, 142*
Erigeron karvinskianus (Santa Barbara daisies), 28
Eschscholzia (California poppy), *12, 34, 71*
Eupatorium (Joe Pye weed), **179**
Euphorbia (spurge), **180**
Evening primrose (*Oenothera*), *70,* **209**

Page numbers in **bold** indicate the Encyclopedia entry for that plant. Numbers in *italics* indicate photographs.

Page numbers in **bold** indicate the Encyclopedia entry for that plant. Numbers in *italics* indicate photographs.